A Program
with Purpose

Thoughts on Building a
Successful Volleyball Program

Johan Dulfer

ISBN: 1483953807

ISBN 13: 9781483953809

Contents

Acknowledgments

Coaching is an incredible profession. It's also an unbelievably stressful one, with highs and lows not always found in other careers, but I can't think of anything more rewarding than to work with a group of young, dedicated individuals toward a goal that we all share. I'm blessed to have ended up in this profession and I owe a great deal of gratitude to Dr. Mike Hebert and Disa Garner for getting me started on the right track. They helped me define my coaching philosophy and find my voice in the gym. I will forever be grateful to both of them. I also owe a tremendous thank you to Steve Yianoukos and Laurel Kane for supporting me when Clarkson's road to success still seemed muddy and uphill. They allowed me to lead this program in the direction we chose. Also, a thank you goes out to Steve Clarke for his help with the editing process. Lastly, this manuscript would have never made it to paper if it hadn't been for the support and encouragement of Avery Marzulla, the love of my life.

To Golden Knights past and present: Thank you for letting me be a part of your tradition and for giving me your all.

Preface

They say that luck favors the prepared. If that's true then maybe there's some hope for me because I'm not normally very lucky. I once was so excited that I had won a parakeet in a coloring contest organized by a pet store, but when we went to pick it up, they had decided to change the prize to a box of crayons. And in the last volleyball match of my senior year, which happened to be the deciding match for the conference championship, I hit an overpass on championship point...seven feet out of bounds. My point is that if the prepared have more luck than those who are winging it, then I'm all for it because prepared is one thing I try to always be. After all, I need all the help available trying to build a volleyball program at a hockey school in the remoteness of Northern New York.

In 2006, after an abysmal first season during which we were lucky to win 7 matches, but also lost 25 of them, it was time to re-evaluate where my new program was going. Out of fifteen available players on the roster, two had graduated and eight had either quit or been told to leave. My office was a revolving door of players coming in crying because they "*just couldn't do it anymore.*" But the true extent of our predicament didn't hit me until the only five (!) remaining players came in together one day in March and asked me "*coach, with only five players, are we even going to have a team next year?*" What do you do when your team doesn't think your program will survive? I did the only thing I could do: I looked them in the eye and assured them "*yes, absolutely...and we're going to win*".

Six years later, as I'm writing this in December of 2012, we have just completed our deepest run into the NCAA tournament in the history of the University – winning our third conference championship in the last four years, capturing our first regional championship and playing in the Elite Eight in the process. It was our fourth consecutive NCAA Tournament appearance for a team that had previously been as far away from the national play-off picture as Anchorage is from Miami Beach. I have to pinch myself from time to time when I think about how far we have come from the days of five returning players, only six years ago. This book is my attempt to write down some of the things that I believe in, and that have been a constant factor in our gym and our program during the past seven seasons.

There are many reasons why Clarkson University has the odds stacked against it from a volleyball perspective. Our location isn't easily accessible, Northern New York offers virtually no high level volleyball of any kind to draw talent from, Clarkson is a very selective school that not just anyone can get into, and volleyball has historically not been a sport of emphasis at our school, where hockey is king. Looking at those odds, it would make no sense for us to have accomplished what we did. So perhaps it's worth exploring some of the decisions and beliefs that allowed us to rise above the expectations. My background is in sport psychology and this book is laced with that viewpoint.

It is my hope that this relatively unique perspective contributes to the existing literature available to coaches. Looking at what's out there, I realize there are a lot of books filled with favorite drills and suggestions on training technique. This is not that kind of book, although there will be some drills included. It is also not a book that's concerned with what level you coach at. Having coached at and experienced high school, club and the highest collegiate level in both Europe as well as the US, I'm convinced that the general tendencies described in this book hold true at all levels. What makes a champion is not just about how tall you are or even how high you jump. Champions exist at every level of play and physical ability and championships are won in areas that sometimes have very little to do with technical volleyball ability and a lot more with the psychological part of the game.

All I'm hoping to do by writing down my experiences is outline a way to think about structuring a program and a team, especially if that way of thinking deviates from the mainstream. I'm not the best coach in the game, and we certainly aren't the most talented team out there. Our drills aren't special by any means, but the way we approach them might be.

Introduction

Playing with Purpose

It was our first-ever championship match. For 34 years, no Clarkson team had ever done better than a middle of the pack finish in the league. We were playing in the conference tournament in Poughkeepsie, NY on Vassar's home court and the last match would decide the league title. As fate would have it, we played the undefeated home team in that last match– not great odds by any means. Oh, and we had just lost the first set. It was now the end of the second set, but we had created our first lead at 21-19. Vassar had just called a time-out and here we were, together in a huddle…10 players looking at me to tell them how to win this set, and get ourselves back in the match. For a moment, my assistant Alesia and I contemplated calming them down. We thought about telling them what so many coaches have told so many teams in time outs over the years: "*It's ok, guys. Take a deep breath; it's just a game – we can do this – first to 25.*" Sound familiar? But this season was different – and so was this time-out.

Twenty eager eyes were piercing me: nervous, anxious and not sure about how to handle this situation. This was new territory for them and for our program. Were they really going to buy it if I tried to tell them it was just another game? The advice of one of my early mentors, national championship coach Klaas Gansevoort of the Netherlands came to mind. "*Match point in the fifth*", he told me once, "*is not a time to calm down and take a deep breath, it's a time to kick it up a notch.*"

Who were we kidding? "*Listen up, ladies*", I told them. "*I'm sure many coaches, including me, have told you to take a deep breath and just play the game when things were tight. They tried to tell you it was just another game against a team like so many others. But here's the truth: That's all a load of crap! We are in a championship match, above 20 points. This is the most important moment of the match. No one in your uniform has ever been in this moment – and we are not letting this chance slip away. Doesn't it feel great? The biggest opportunity of your career is here. Embrace it. We need to take control of the match and I believe you can do it. So when their #13 takes another swing in the middle, I want us to take away left back. Serve tough and attack the 5/6 seam. Go get it*". My team roared out of the time-out and never looked back, winning the next three sets and winning our first-ever league championship.

Sometimes in order to go where you've never gone before, you've got to do what you've never done before. That time-out was one of those moments. It made sense to acknowledge the pressure of the situation and use it in our favor. Pressure is part of the game. Why should we avoid it? This team had known all season that they would be in a position to challenge for a championship and pointing out the situation in that time-out just made them aware that they were on the verge of accomplishing their goal. Pointing out the magnitude of the situation ironically actually calmed them down.

The motto of the Clarkson University women's volleyball program is *"some people see things as they are and ask "why" – we dream of things that never were and ask "why not?"* It's the most powerful quote I know. George Bernard Shaw could have been a coach or a sport psychologist for his insight into how big changes happen. It starts with a goal, a vision...with purpose.

In fact, that little word, *purpose*, is by far the most used word in our gym culture. I am the type of coach who will sometimes stop a drill and talk to my players about "purpose" instead of pointing out what exactly went technically wrong in the drill. Sometimes the mindset is what needs adjusting first; not the way you swing your arm or move your feet.

Players tend to look at me oddly when they first hear me go off about having purpose, but gradually they get it. *"When you send in your resume for a job"*, I'll ask them, *"Would you put in a standard letter that's just ok, expecting you'll never hear back anyway? Or do you make sure your CV stands out as much as you can, so that you end up on the top of the pile?* Are you just going through the motions and hoping for a good result, or are you actually *planning* for a good result? Are you preparing to be successful or satisfied with mediocre?

Purpose is such a crucial element, but it can also sound awfully vague. I'm reminded of my first season as a coach, for Club Veracles at the University of Groningen, when I was fond of reminding my teams in time outs to simply "*focus*". It was amazing how incredibly ineffective this was. I might as well have said something like "*we have to be better*" or "*try harder*", equally meaningless phrases. So in our gym, we have worked on defining the concept of "purpose" to the point where the players know what we mean by it.

<u>Purpose is the reasoning behind your decision-making. It's your goal, your ideal outcome – your master plan.</u> The key to purpose is to know *why* you make the decisions you make and standing by them.

If you're an outside hitter in my gym, you might have to be ready to be asked why you hit a certain shot. Or why you just served zone 5. My liberos frequently get asked *why* they were reading a certain direction, and I'm sure I drive my setter crazy with inquiries about her decision-making.

Purpose should define most if not all steps of building a program and coaching a team. It is found (I would hope) in all the building blocks of our program. These building blocks include vision for the program, communication, confidence building and goal setting, building a support structure, recruiting, and lastly, but certainly not least importantly, the tactical (and technical) choices within the game itself.

1

Program Vision

It was clear early on that we were (and maybe we will always be) the underdogs. Coaches usually like that situation – it's a good position to be in. Underdogs want to win. They're not expected to, but they desperately crave victory over the favorite. But is that enough? In my opinion, the single victory is not enough to sustain success. Program building should be concerned with what happens after the first upset...the matter of what happened to David after Goliath fell to his knees. What next? Your vision is what you want your program to achieve over time. It is the plan you set in place to achieve the upset, but is must also include the plan to sustain that success and build upon it.

The Building Blocks of Vision

As coaches, we have to ask ourselves what the building blocks of our vision are. What do you want your program to stand for, and what do you want your teams and players to be known for? Among the questions that have to be answered is what brand of volleyball you'll be bringing to the floor. In other words: Ask yourself what the key to success is going to be for your program and team. Another question to ask yourself is what type of leadership you want. For example, what sort of coaching style will you be using (and will it change depending on your team?). Also important are what ethical standards you want your teams to adhere to. This also refers to what work ethic and energy level will be demanded in practice and games. Fourth, you'll have to decide what types of players you'll be recruiting (talent and personality) and the people you're going to be surrounding yourself with. The fifth building block of vision is your ability to act as if you've already achieved your vision. In addition to talking the talk, you have to walk the walk.

1. Pick your Brand

In the movie "Miracle", which at one point we've all watched with our teams, coach Herb Brooks tells his team, that *"the legs feed the wolf"*.

Coach Brooks believed that if his team was going to be outmatched in talent, they were going to make up for it in being better prepared physically. I believe that in order to build a successful program, you have to start by envisioning the brand of volleyball you'd like to play. What is your team going to be good at, and how are you going to win matches? When all is said and done, the outcome that your program is measured by is wins, and it's our job as coaches to figure out how we're going to create those wins.

<u>My philosophy has always been that your odds of winning a volleyball match go up depending on how good you are at maximizing your aggressiveness while minimizing your errors.</u>

If you can push your opponent into the uncomfortable situation that they commit more errors than you do, you're going to have a great chance of success. This may sound logical, but I find that many coaches seem to think that it's always necessary to be stronger, taller and more athletic than an opponent to win. This is not the case. There is a strong argument to be made for just being smarter.

At the very top level of our game, it might be true that the best athletes make the difference. After all, it's hard to argue against the benefit of having a few Destinee Hookers on your team. But at the Division III level (as well as most other levels I have coached at), I would argue for volleyball IQ over physical prowess any day of the week. Especially if I had to pick one or the other. Obviously a combination of the two would be ideal, but given the choice, I would take the smarter, more polished player over the taller, stronger and physically more gifted player without experience every time, at least as a starting point to build a program. With the limited contact hours we are allowed in Division III, this decision is made even easier. There simply isn't usually enough time in the gym to turn a high-error player into a low error asset.

My first year at Clarkson, I was lucky enough to inherit a good setter, who came in as a freshman that year. Even without this lucky circumstance, I would encourage anyone to start building a team from the setter position. First, with a good setter, the quality of your passes magically becomes higher. Good setters change mediocre passes into good ones, and bad passes into mediocre ones. Second, having a good setter on your team allows you to go out and recruit hitters by telling them they should want to play with this setter, who will get them a great set.

While most coaches would agree on the importance of a good setter as the foundation of a team, I think most would then pick a great outside hitter as their second building block. I disagree. It's not that I don't think a great outside hitter will help you win matches; I do. But I think if faced with a choice, I would pick an outstanding libero first. Given my philosophy that the team that commits fewer errors wins the majority of the matches, it makes sense to try to force opponents into beating themselves before they can beat you. By that I mean, if you dig enough balls and send them back over the net, and you pass well enough to be in system a good amount of time, it forces your opponent to be clean and effective in order to beat you; or, at the very least, cleaner than you. Not many teams can do that on a consistent basis. Most teams implode if put under enough pressure, especially if you also add strong serving.

The added advantage of prioritizing recruiting a great libero, is that this position is under-scholarshipped in division II and division I. Most teams will have three to four outside hitters on scholarship, but usually only one libero. This means that there are lots of defensive specialists out there who are good enough to make a difference at our level, whom I can recruit without having to compete with a scholarship offer.

Next, I would choose an outside hitter who can keep the ball in play while being aggressive. Ideally, this player is a good passer and defender as well, because that adds to the game plan that we started by recruiting the libero. At Clarkson, our first outside hitter to make a difference was really a defensive specialist. She wasn't the big gun on the outside that put balls away with her powerful arm swing, but she was the tool and change-up player who hit a rather low .128 for the season. Her hitting percentage wasn't low because she made a lot of errors, but because she didn't put down a lot of kills. She took between 50 and 70 swings a match and kept most of them in play. We weren't going to win if a team played their best against us. But if you didn't, we were going to wear you down by simply attempting to make fewer mistakes than you. We passed better by now, set pretty cleanly, and put a lot of balls back in play. By the end of the season, our outside hitter was the school record holder for number of kills in a season, but her shoulder had almost fallen off in the process because of how many swings she had taken to accomplish that feat. We weren't very good yet, but we had turned the corner and we were now beating teams we hadn't beaten in a long time.

Next came adding the middle game and finding a right side to help out. All the while, we kept adding height to the program. Our front row in those years was an average height of 5'7 across the board, middle hitters included. They were all scrappy athletes who fought their hearts out every match and just wouldn't quit. From there, we could start plugging the holes in our system. First up was recruiting outside hitters who could help us put balls away at a higher clip, so we could start forcing wins instead of just hoping to stay in games.

Throughout all of this, I always keep my eye out for one very important factor: the ability of players to serve the ball consistently and aggressively. I'll talk more about our serving philosophy in the chapter on tactical choices of the game, but if I have to choose between two similar players, the one who serves the best always gets the nod. It's a win-win. Good servers create better passers in your own gym, and they create chaos for your opponent.

The order of this process is likely different for every coach, because all of us have different beliefs about the game. That's why it has to start with identifying those beliefs and working from there to find your personnel. Dr. Mike Hebert, a coaching legend, once told me he thought coaching was "*creating your own universe*", and he was right.

2. Leadership

They say that a leader without followers is just someone taking a walk. So when you look over your shoulder, is there anyone there? Are you taking a walk by yourself, or is your team right behind you?

There are all sorts of leaders. There are leaders by example, and there are vocal leaders. There are autocratic leaders and there are participative leaders. Leadership is a flexible concept and that's a good thing because it allows us to develop our own style, matched to the group (or team) we wish to lead.

Coaching Style

I have adjusted my coaching style over the years, as I'm sure you have. If you're still the same coach you were five years ago, then I encourage you to talk to your team and evaluate a little. Some of my teams needed different things than other teams and every year is a new challenge. When I first got started at Clarkson, it was important to set the bar high and make it clear that there was a new sheriff in town. My coaching style was much more autocratic than it is now. By autocratic I mean that decisions were made by me alone. My players weren't really allowed input into any decisions and I ruled with an iron fist. That was needed at the time, because we had to find out who would stick around for the right reasons and who would decide it wasn't for them. But it's no longer how I coach. I have changed as my teams have evolved. I've evolved into a more participative decision maker. I would think that my brothers will run into that soon as their daughters, my nieces, get older. When you're 15 and thinking of dating your first tattooed drummer, you need a different type of "leadership" than when you're 18 and heading off to college. Dad's shotgun might have to be replaced by mom's care package.

It has been shown that the higher the level of a women's team, the more the women on the team prefer a typical "male" coaching style, meaning a more autocratic style. But it has also been shown that teams that learn to deal effectively with conflict and issues generally have coaches with a more democratic coaching style.

I am lucky in the sense that as college coaches we are able to try to find good matches for the coaching style that we prefer through recruiting. But regardless, every year is a process of evolution. The goal is to lead a team effectively and it always takes some adjusting to make it work. Do I need to yell more? Do I need to be giving more praise? Are the captains capable of handling team conflict or do I need to be more involved? All of those decisions factor into what type of leader a coach can and should be during a season. But no matter how good a job we do as coaches, we need our players to be leaders as well.

At Clarkson, there is a heavy emphasis on developing leaders. An unusually high percentage of Clarkson graduates go on to lead a company or business in the first few years after graduation, and it makes sense that an understanding of responsibility would also lend itself well to taking charge on the volleyball court. I believe in helping my team develop the leadership they need amongst each other.

The Pygmalion Coach

Some players undoubtedly have more potential to lead than others. Sometimes there seems to be no desire to lead and sometimes we may not see any potential. And sometimes players think they would be good leaders and the coaching staff disagrees. Ultimately, leadership roles should go to those players who are well respected and best integrated in the team fabric. Do they need to be the captains?

Every year I wonder how the selection of captains will go for my team. If you're like me, you've held your breath as well, as the team voted on who will represent them as captains. Will it be a popularity contest, or will we actually end up with the captains that we think will be the best at their jobs? I have always allowed my teams to vote on the honor of captains, and most years I have not been disappointed. I'm lucky that my players have learned to distinguish between the good of the program and the good of the individual. But there have definitely been "*uh-oh, I hope that this will work out– moments*" along the way. The knife cuts both ways. On the one hand, we could end up with less-than-qualified captains, while on the other we could end up having to deal with disgruntled athletes who were not selected and had hoped to be.

To put the results of the captain election in perspective, I think it's important to keep one thing in mind. For years, I told my teams that the first priority of the captain is to be the buffer between the coaching staff and the team. To be the extension of the coaching staff in the locker room and on the court. But I now have a slightly different view. I still think that captains should have their fingers on the pulse of the team and be in charge of bringing things to the coaches' attention if it's warranted. And I certainly believe that good captains guard the locker room culture. But in terms of communication with the coaches, I think it's fair to say that if I'm solely relying on my captains to relay my message to the team, I'm probably in trouble. The trust and openness that is a requirement for a participative leadership style has to be present with all (or most) members of my team. Not just the captains.

Coaches' Favorites

We have to be careful to avoid letting our preconceived notions about leadership potential get in the way of developing the leadership we want. A 1968 study called "Pygmalion in the Classroom" points out what I mean by that[1]. In the study, teachers were told at the beginning of the school year that a certain group of students they were working with consisted of "late bloomers" who had potential for huge academic and intellectual gains during the school year. In actuality, the kids were selected at random. At the end of the year, however, the kids in the "high potential" group had actually achieved greater gains than the kids in the group that had not been identified as high potential. You can imagine that this affected feedback as well. The whole thing turns into a self-fulfilling prophecy.

The Pygmalion coach concept easily transfers to our coaching on the court as well. Every coach has at some point been accused of playing favorites. I hear it often from recruits when I ask them about their current coaches and so I'm sure it's been said about me: "*Coach likes Kelly better than me*". If you're like me, you probably have no idea where those ideas come from because most coaches don't deliberately play favorites.

---

1   Sternberg Horn, T, Lox, C and Labrador, F. The self-fulfilling prophecy theory: when coaches' expectations become reality. In: Williams, J. (Ed). Applied Sport Psychology: personal growth to peak performance (2001) (Fourth Edition). Mountain View, CA (Mayfield). P. 63.

During one of the more difficult moments in the first few years at Clarkson, one of my athletes once gave me a printout of a story she thought would make me feel better. It was of a high school coach admitting he had favorites. His favorites, he said, were the players who stayed after practice to work on their skills, the athletes who worked hard without complaining; the players who were courteous and asked questions, the players who never made excuses and the players who went the extra mile. He said that those players deserved to get extra attention and help, because giving that help to the players that did not behave in appropriate ways would be rewarding the wrong behavior. He invited all of his athletes to become his favorites.

Receiving this write-up from my player made me feel better because she was one of those players who "*got it*". She had seen me be accused of favoring someone and didn't think it was fair. While I appreciated her gesture, the incident has made me very aware of how much attention I spend on which athlete and when. I'm much more aware of it now than I was then. After all, sometimes we just don't realize the message we're sending. We could be spending extra energy on the player who is asking for extra help or with the player who continues to sabotage practices – no matter the reason behind it, the reality is that we are observed as spending extra energy on these athletes. That opens the door for interpretation: *Coach likes Kelly better.* Are we playing favorites? Are we rewarding the wrong behavior? Or are we simply doing our jobs without thinking about the message we send?

Let me give you an example of how we're sometimes not aware of the message we're sending. I have two cats that I love dearly. Now by no means does my wife Avery have to worry about her place in the pecking order in our household. But Gonzo and Ernie tend to demand a lot of attention. They usually are doing something cute, warranting me to talk to them, pick them up, pet them and play with them.

One day, my wife was sitting on the couch as I engaged in my usual "*oh you're so cute*" ritual with the kitties. As I baby-talked to my two furry friends, she looked at me and just said "*meow*". She has a way of making great points with very few words.

My point is that it's important to strike a good balance between rewarding the right behavior and avoiding spending too much time on the "squeaky wheels". Sometimes appearance is everything and we have to think about the message we send.

Stewardship

So why is it important to encourage athlete participation in the (leadership) process and appear fair as you're coaching your team? It all starts with a sense of ownership of the program. We refer to the volleyball team as "*our program*" and there's a reason for that. I want the players who come in to help me to continue to make the program better. Not just in terms of the number of wins we have each year (although that would be nice), but as an overall product. We want to do the right thing and be seen as examples and role models off the court as well as on the court.

In essence, I want my players to leave the program better than when they found it. By giving them a sense of ownership in the program, it is my hope that what they leave behind will give them a sense of pride that will outlast any championship or playoff appearance.

I want my athletes to lead, step up and take ownership. And the best way to do that, is to make sure that they know it's their own program that is at stake. I want them to be true stewards of the program. Let me put it a different way. There is bird poop on my car, on the sidewalk, and on my window at work. Once, when I was sitting on a bench in a park in Barcelona, a dove pooped on my head. Birds will drop their poop anywhere anytime. But one place where you'll never find it is in their own nests. It works the same way with volleyball players.

3. Ethical Standards

A championship level team has to live up to its reputation off the court as well. There are expectations that come along with being a champion. The French call it "*noblesse oblige*" – which roughly translates as "with nobility comes expectation". It's hard enough to define what you want the expectations to be, let alone deciding what standards to adhere to when you're not at the championship level yet. I believe that there should be no difference between the two. If you expect your team to become a winner, then you should hold them accountable according to a winner's standards. And this applies to the coaching staff as well.

This is, of course, easier said than done. On most campuses around the country there is sometimes evidence of athletes getting away with poor behavior. Occasionally this is because coaches refuse to act when rules are broken, but a lot of the time it's simply because as coaches we are unaware of team rules being broken. When my athletes see others get away with poor behavior, they must sometimes wonder why I'm on them so much about maintaining their discipline. My answer is always that in order to be extraordinary *on* the court, you have to be extraordinary *off* the court, too. You have to be different from everyone else. My hope is that if I can get them to buy into the concept of being different (and extraordinary), they will accept the fact that our standards might in some ways be higher than those of other teams or of the general student population. The problem of course is how to police the standards you set as a team.

In my opinion, it's crucial to start out being absolutely ruthless in applying penalties, even if it hurts the outcome of games. There is no substitute for players seeing you're willing to risk as much as a win (or several wins) to honor the standards of the program. As coaches we are dependent on the collective decisions of a group of 18 to 22 year olds. Although my players are certainly better than average decision makers and I trust them a great deal, it's scary how much of what goes on off the court we are probably not aware of. The fact is, though, that I sleep better at night knowing that my athletes know there will be absolutely no leniency if violations of our rules come to my attention.

There is a lot of literature on how to create team rules. Some coaches are fans of creating a rulebook almost as big as an NFL playbook while others prefer to stick to a limited number of rules.

The advantage of trying to capture every possible scenario in a rulebook is that there is little grey area. I know coaches who have to dedicate an entire afternoon in preseason just taking their team through the binder with the team rules. The meetings usually cover everything from curfew, travel protocol, to the use of chewing gum in the gym, to acceptable tattoos and body piercings. While it certainly drives home the point that there are boundaries and they are to be respected, I always wonder if the players are thinking about what they've gotten themselves into while sitting through these meetings. I'm not sure it sends a message of mutual trust. The other downside, of course, is that if a situation arises that is not covered by the rulebook, your hands could be tied. If you're telling your team that the rulebook is all-inclusive, then anything not covered is fair game.

In my opinion it is impossible to cover all of your bases, which is why some coaches only use one rule – usually some variation of "*do the right thing*". Those coaches choose to be flexible and trust that the team can distinguish between what is right and wrong. It is my opinion that teenagers crave discipline and structure, but not to the extent that their every move is predicted and outlined, with consequences and all. We choose to keep a list of 6-8 rules that we feel strongly about, and leave the rest open-ended by asking everyone to do the right thing. Below are the rules as we use them at Clarkson.

Clarkson Team Rules:

1. I will be on time (by being early)
2. I will work hard to solve team issues within the team fabric, never airing "dirty laundry" outside of that team fabric
3. I will go to class – no excuses
4. I will support my teammates at all times (even when I'm not on the court)
5. I will abide by a "24 hour rule"
6. No alcohol with recruits – ever.
7. I will represent Clarkson in a positive light (which also means attempting to eliminate profanity on and off the court)
8. In case of a perceived conflict, I will go straight to the source instead of assuming and spreading rumors. I will also encourage others to do the same.
9. With the best interest of the future of the program in mind, I will <u>do the right thing!</u>

Some coaches get their teams involved in creating the rules, whereas others list the rules and don't allow input. I like to have a meeting with my team in preseason and to ask them if they can live with the rules. Most of them haven't changed in quite a while so the players are familiar with them and have enforced them (or seen them enforced) over the years, which makes my job easier. During the meeting we clarify the rules and ask everyone to sign the document to symbolize we're all literally on the same page. I especially like to get my team (or the captains) involved in handing out fair punishment when needed. I find that oftentimes, they are tougher on themselves than I could ever be. I remember wanting to suspend a player for three weeks once for an alcohol infraction, and the team captains suggested five weeks. As surprised as I was, it's not strange to me that they care that much about the program and its foundation. And in this particular case, I was glad to be the "good cop" for a change by suspending the player for four weeks.

Whatever path you follow in creating your team's list of standards, I urge you to forge the link between the rules (standards) and the championship behavior you wish to model.

Punishment, in this scenario, is not just punishing for violating the rule, but for something much bigger: for failing to act like a champion – for letting the team down. I don't think it is a coincidence that in my first three seasons at Clarkson, I had to put out more fires than I wanted to, and that we weren't winning any championships (yet). It resulted in several long suspensions, and more than a few players (and a coach) that had to be cut from the team. I was ruthless with punishment, but caring and diligent in explaining the reasoning behind it. I also don't think it is a coincidence that in the four years since then we have had relatively few issues to deal with and we've won a lot more.

4. Choose your Followers

That first year at Clarkson, my recruiting assignment was simple: find better players. But how do you get someone to commit to a program that just went 7-25 and only has 5 players left?

I didn't have time to think about it. All we did was talk to as many players as we could about coming in and helping make a difference.

Of course, when I was going out looking for new players that first year, I wasn't able to get the "studs", the difference makers, just yet. I needed to focus on getting the right building blocks in place: the passing and low error volleyball I talked about earlier. I remember losing one of the top recruits in the state, a 5'9 outside hitter with a bullet for a serve and a great vertical leap, to an already established program mainly because she wasn't sure I could guarantee her she wouldn't be the best player in the program from day one. I couldn't, because she would have been. Ironically, she went to play for a school where she also ended up being the best player and a three-time All-American, but I understood her concern nonetheless.

Five years later, I can go out and talk to players about coming to play for a team that was within 3 wins of a national title and all of them know that they're coming into a well-established group of dedicated athletes. Different doors open at different times.

My first recruiting class at Clarkson was the first class to make it to an NCAA tournament – in their senior year. When I asked them that year if they remembered what had made them come to Clarkson, all three of them told me honestly that they would've never come if they had looked a little more closely at the previous year's record. They told me all they could think about was the vision I had described to them, and they simply failed to do enough research on the state of the program at the time. I had gotten lucky from the sound of it, but it shows how the vision for a successful future should always trump the memory of an unsuccessful past.

I also believe that building a program cannot simply start with recruiting volleyball talent alone. You need a combination of the skills you're looking for and the attitude to match the state of your program. If you're an established power, the players you're looking at will need to be equipped with different psychological traits than if you're storming the gates of the volleyball world. The best example I can think of is the players that ended up playing for me despite what seemed like my best efforts to turn them against me.

You see, I have told many players that they weren't as good as they thought they were, or informed them about things about their game they needed to work on. Of course, this may not be the best way to woo recruits. Many recruiters I know spend their days telling teenagers how great they are and how great of a fit for their program. While this is certainly important (after all, you want them to come play for you) I have also gotten lucky finding a few gems that ended up playing for me simply to prove me wrong. They appreciated my honesty about their game and figured honest feedback was going to make them better.

Sometimes I'm still baffled when I think about how that worked, but I'll take a player with a chip on their shoulder any day over one who's been told she's the best thing since sliced bread. Come to think of it, I have a roster full of them. Most of my players were told by Division I and II coaches that they'd be back-up players or role players at best. They were too short, or didn't jump high enough in the opinion of these coaches. All of them came to play for me to prove to themselves they could do more than others had told them they'd be able to do.

Their attitude matches the program's and mine. With all of its built-in disadvantages, Clarkson as a volleyball program is in the same boat. All of us refuse to buy into what common sense tells us: that a hockey school in Northern NY, specializing in the science field cannot be a major contender in volleyball. In my world, that's a recipe for success. After all: Those who say it cannot be done should not interrupt the person doing it!

5. Act as If

They say that if you don't know where you're going, any road will take you there. But how would you know?

The truth is, if you don't know where you're going, you'll never know if you've reached your destination. Too many underdogs are in this predicament. They hope to come out on top, but it remains just that: hope. If you're building a program, you've got to plan to make it. You have to see what the results of that labor look like in your mind's eye. Some would say *"fake it until you make it"*, but there's nothing fake about it. You have to live it and breathe it every day, and –perhaps most importantly- you have to get others to buy into it. Every year I do this little exercise for myself. I write down a prediction of the next four years. They are very succinct descriptions of how the year will go, who has a chance to be award winners, what goals the team accomplishes and who are the carrying players. At the end of every season, I review these crystal ball write-ups from a few years ago and check to see how far off I was. If things fall into place, you'll see that they won't be too far off reality. For us, it's been fun to send these things to recruits to point out to them that there is a plan in place for their development and success and it's more than just a wish.

Vision Shared

If you keep your vision to yourself, it's just a dream. I believe in sharing what you're planning and how you're planning on getting there with anyone who wants to hear it. It's the only way to get help along the way and to get support built behind the scenes.

In the 2009 season we played a seasoned NCAA-tournament team in our opening match of the year. We lost the match 1-3, but several points into it, my assistant and I looked at each other and knew this season would be different. We were physical, intense, and smart...playing a great match. My team knew it, too, and there was a feeling of confidence with us all weekend long. On the second day we ended up beating the previous year's champion from our conference in non-conference action, and that confirmed our hunch. We were going to have a chance to challenge for our first conference championship that season. Two weeks later, the campus TV station asked to interview three of my players, and they were almost giddy during the interview. I can't blame them; they finally had a lot to be excited about. But when the interviewer asked them what the future would hold for them, my girls were afraid to jinx themselves, and answered that they had a "secret goal" within the team, which they were hoping to accomplish. I knew that the secret goal was an NCAA tournament berth, the first in school history. But it wasn't a secret. I had to have a conversation with my team about being absolutely clear in what you're trying to accomplish, and that it's ok and even necessary to share it with the world. After all, when you shout from the rooftops what you're planning on doing, you'd better give it your all to make it, or everyone will know you failed. Pressure is a healthy motivator for those who are determined and able.

2

Communication

Coaching requires communication in so many ways. The way you think about your program and your team will inevitably impact the way you talk with your players, and also how you deal with your administration and fans. But have you thought about how you communicate with *yourself*?

Purpose is Affirmative

If I asked you not to think about a purple elephant, you would likely not be able to get it out of your head. And what if I specifically told you the elephant has yellow dots and is wearing a white tutu? Admit it, you have ballet-dancing elephants on your mind right now, don't you? In order for you to avoid thinking about the dancing elephant, I'm much better off telling you what I *do* want you to think about. In our gym, I believe in telling a player to keep her elbow high, rather than telling her not to drop her elbow. I'll tell a player to serve zone 6, instead of asking her to "*not miss anymore serves*". And I'll ask my assistant coach to come up with a weakness in a defense before the next time-out, rather than commenting to her that "*we have to stop getting dug*".

Purpose is saying what you want. But purpose is also defining the way in which you want it, and the timeline that you have in mind.

Purposeful communicating implies you have those goals in mind. If that's the case, then –for me- it makes sense that our communication is mostly positive. It has been shown that athletes remember negative feedback much better than positive feedback. This is of course true for anyone. If you're brave, you can experiment on your spouse. Try giving him or her five compliments, followed by the statement "*but those pants make you look fat*", and see which of the six comments they'll focus on. Although it can sometimes feel great to unleash a negative comment after yet another missed assignment, research has shown that it takes multiple positive remarks to overcome one single negative comment. Just think about how much effort it would take you to get out of the doghouse for the pants comment – that's exactly how it works with feedback on the court as well.

As much as we want to express our frustrations when our outside hitter misses on three swings in a row, there is unmistakable power of purpose in "*I love how high your elbow was on that swing. Next time, if you also get your feet to the ball, you'll crush the 3 meter line.*" You may have to take a deep breath to have these words come out of your mouth, but the results will not lie.

Embracing the elephant in the room

At the beginning of our season in 2012, we were getting ready for our season opener against nationally ranked Springfield College. The Pride, ranked #21 in the national preseason poll, had just come off an appearance in the national quarterfinals the season before, and had beaten us solidly in our gym that year. They were a very good and experienced team. My team, on the other hand, consisted of four starting freshmen, none of whom had any collegiate experience at all. I had started preseason like any other preseason: by talking about our goal of winning a championship. I had told the team that *at some point* this season they were going to be facing the opportunity to knock off a favored opponent, or win a championship, or both. I kept hammering the point home those first two weeks of practices. I'd stop drills and talk about purpose. "*When we get to that moment*", I'd ask them, "*will you be ready?*" I even told them the story of our first championship and the time-out that started it all. "*Many coaches, including me, have told you that it's just a game...but that's a load of crap*"...

By the time we got on the bus to Springfield for our opening match, they were probably sick of it. "*Yes, yes, we know...we are going to be in big moments...*"

Little did I know, that one of those moments would arrive as early as that evening. When we walked into the gym, Springfield was playing their opening match of the tournament. We watched them beat their opponents, but I remember thinking they looked beatable. Of course, it's my job to think that everyone is beatable so I wondered what my players were thinking. We still hadn't played as much as a set together in a match that mattered, and Springfield was working out the early season kinks right in front of us and would surely be ready for us.

The match started predictably. We struggled to find a rhythm in the first set, because it was our first match of the season and it was the first collegiate match ever for four of our six starters. But we kept it close and somehow grew into the match. After two hours of grueling play, we found ourselves tied 2-2. A fifth set, in our first match of the year, against a ranked opponent. I could sense the nerves, and the excitement all at the same time. Emotions were raging and I needed to find a way to put it all in perspective for my team. I'll let you guess what I told them in the huddle, after handing in the lineup for the fifth set.

"*Ladies*", I smiled, "*many coaches, including me, have told you…*" I didn't even need to finish the sentence. Huge smiles greeted me as I looked around the huddle, and they all burst out in unison: "*That's a load of crap!*" Instead of trying to relax by denying the pressures of the moment, acknowledging pressure moments for what they are, and making them familiar moments, or moments you were expecting, can help deal with the stress.

Experience is the key to being comfortable under stress. My team instantly relaxed as they noticed that this was what we had talked about for two whole weeks. We jumped out to a good lead and never gave it up, beating our first ranked opponent of the season in five sets on their home floor to start the year.

Those time-outs were of course not anything special. I didn't invent the concept of being honest and upfront with my team in a moment of pressure. It was a choice we made as coaches, in the heat of the moment, not to allow our team to diminish the moment but instead encouraging them to embrace the pressure and rise above it. Winning our first championship and beating our first ranked opponent were our goals and it gave us a purpose: to play every point as if it were championship point. If you want big moments to bring out the best in you, then the first step is to recognize and embrace those moments; not hide from them and hope for the best.

Have you ever wondered how to get players ready for those big moments? Maybe you're like me and you've tried the drills that put the score at 21-21 and play out the last four points and maybe you, too, have found that it never really works that way. Two missed serves and two passing errors later, my players never really seemed to get the point that we were practicing the big points. To them, those drills were always just drills. They failed to mimic the stress of a match or the size of the moment. It was always just practice and after one drill many more would follow, and they knew it.

So I've started spelling it out for them in different ways. I'll stop a scrimmage in the middle, point out the score, and ask the next server if she's up to her task. I'll tell her, in front of all of her teammates, that if she scores, she wins the game, but if she misses, the game is over...and ask her if she's ready to serve an ace, putting all kinds of pressure on her. Of course, you have to be somewhat careful whom you select for these little exercises, but if done well, they work. I'll let her serve and then after the rally, we'll evaluate. If it was in, I'll praise her for doing well under pressure and not letting me get to her. If she misses, I'll do damage control by pointing out the good elements of the serve. She was either obviously trying to serve it to a certain zone, or it had a lot of speed to it. All things we needed at a crucial time. I'll praise the purpose of the serve.

Slowly but surely, I am hoping my players get it. They can be called on at any time so they'd better be ready to perform. Just like the game requires in tight moments. You never know who will serve on match point for a championship.

Speak up, or forever suffer the consequences

Dealing with conflict might be the hardest thing I have to do in my job. So much of our job as coaches depends on the team staying together and walking in the same direction. But conflict and issues are bound to come up, threatening the team resolve. Communication with purpose is always the answer.

It is said that women have a hard time confronting each other with issues. I've been told that if you have teenage daughters and only one bathroom in your house, you may not be inclined to believe this right away, but it's true. Women are peacemakers, and sometimes tend to ignore issues and trouble and hope those might go away without being addressed. Coaching women is completely different from coaching men in many ways, and one of the most challenging things about coaching a women's team has to be how to keep everyone on board and bought into the same goals. This can be especially challenging for a male coaching females, because our experience is usually that issues get talked about a little quicker. Men will generally not let anything fester, will bring it up sooner but will then also forgive and forget quicker.

The outside hitter on my own college team was one of my best friends, but you hadn't been yelled at until you made a mistake in his eyes. After the match, however, we'd have a drink together and (hopefully) celebrate the win and forget all about the outbursts on the court. It was all business, and nothing personal. Women, on the other hand, tend to not let go quite as easily and grudges might be held a bit longer.

Most of my players will tell me that they are afraid that airing their concerns with their teammates "*will only make it worse*". I believe that as coaches, it is our job to help alleviate some of these fears, and teach our players the benefits of open, honest communication. Without a doubt, teams that go on and have success in the later portion of their season, when championships are won, are teams that overcome their internal issues and team drama.

Most, if not all, of my teams at Clarkson have had a variety of issues to work through. I think most teams do, and it's almost unavoidable if you're going to work together so intensely for about three months. But we choose not to hide from them. In fact, we warn the team on day one of preseason that issues are going to arise and we talk about what those issues might be. Roommate conflict, teammates not working hard enough or dodging workouts, playing time issues, we discuss every likely scenario.

I will then ask my players to describe Tuckman's[2] four stages of team development to me as I write them on the white board. Years ago, I introduced this concept to them, and now I don't have to remind them anymore– the returners know them by heart and the new team members learn them quickly. We just modified Tuckman's original order of the stages a little.

a) Forming

   In this phase the team is being formed. Whether it's through tryouts, or through recruiting, a group of individuals is put together and gets the label "team". It's an exciting phase where everyone is optimistic about the prospect of working together and the sky is the limit. For most of us, this is preseason.

b) Norming

   In this phase the team decides the rules by which it wants to live. Players and coaches talk about what's important to them and the team comes up with its identity. Do we have a dry season? Do we allow gossip in the locker room? Will we stand up if someone breaks curfew? Will we have a curfew?

c) Storming

   Second in Tuckman's original theory, I consider the storming phase the third of the four, and taking place a little later in the

---

2   Tuckman, B. (1965). Developmental sequence in small groups. *Psychological Bulletin, 63,* 384–99.

season. Almost all teams eventually hit this storming phase. It's the phase where little things boil over, or big things hit the fan. In my years at Clarkson, this stage has ranged from players fighting, a team captain getting thrown off the team for violating team rules two weeks before the conference post season, players accusing an injured player of dodging workouts, and the common *"she doesn't like me"* arguments. It's completely normal and happens to every team. What matters is how you deal with it and *whether* you come out of it.

d) Performing

This is the last stage of team development. It's also the most difficult stage to reach. Most teams do not make it out of the storming phase and get stuck cycling back and forth between storming and norming. The teams that win championships find ways to get through the storming phase. In fact, it is sometimes suggested that teams *need* to go through a storming phase in order to reach the performing goal.

When I talk to my team in preseason, I will tell them that conflict is going to happen, and that we will have to recognize it and find a way out. I've found that somehow it works reassuring to my teams. They know that things will come up. By making them understand that not only is it normal, it is so normal that a researcher formed an entire four-step theory on it, we try to take away the stress of it all.

It's a good thing to experience turbulence, as long as you recognize it and deal with it effectively. It's the only way to win a championship. I've had several captains' meetings where my captains told me "*don't worry coach, we're just storming; we'll be ok*". In a way, it's the concept of embracing the elephant in the room. By sharing with your team that what they're going through is normal, we can make it understandable and hand them the ability to deal with it.

Of course, this is easier said than done. Some teams simply succumb to the internal strife and never rise above the issues. They get stuck in the storming phase. The most difficult coaching decision is whether and when to intervene.

When my 2012 team started showing signs of storming in late October, my initial instinct was to let them find a solution on their own. The issue was clearly a lack of communication and understanding. Several players had come into my office complaining about the lack of support and dedication of other players. But none of them had approached their teammates directly, thinking it would only make matters worse. I wasn't overly excited to step in right away. There were some awful accusations, but I was convinced that they were just the normal miscommunication issues. So instead of jumping in, I kept encouraging the individual players to communicate and work it out on their own. But by the time I had heard from five players individually, my assistant and I were over it and decided to do something after all.

To start practice one night, we brought everyone into the team room together and had them write the four stages of team development on the white board. I explained to them that from what

I had heard, I was convinced we were in the storming phase. I had heard things that -if true- were a threat to not just this team, but to the program in general and I wasn't going to allow that to happen. In fact, if some of these things were true, I told them some of them might need to rethink their membership on the team. I deliberately stayed very vague so that I wasn't making it a personal attack on anyone, but I saw the shock in their eyes. "*He's going to cut us just because we're not communicating properly?*" "*Is he talking about me?*"

I also quickly added, that I personally thought the issues were actually resolvable, but that they had just been ignored for too long and had gotten out of control. I also told them that what we were about to do was something that had inherent risks for women's teams. We were going to put all of our issues on the table and discuss them.

I told them that there was a chance that my strategy of having them spill their guts in a team meeting would backfire; but that I was counting on their maturity and heart for the team to make it work. It was the kind of team I hoped would respond well to my trust. I wanted them to know I was counting on them to help resolve this. I wanted them to just come out and hash everything out. Then, I laid down the rules:

1. If anything is bothering you, you have to speak up now (speak up, or suffer the consequences)
2. As long as you're describing how you *feel*, no one can argue with you. If you feel that way, that's how you feel. It's much more

fair to say *"you made me feel lonely"* than it is to accuse someone by saying *"you always exclude me on purpose"*
3. Let your teammates talk, and then answer honestly...

I left my assistant coach in the room with them, and had instructed her to make sure that the issues that we were aware of would come to light. Ironically, she never had to intervene. One by one, the girls shared how they felt and what obstacles to our success they were experiencing. Tears were shed but watching team members take turns opening up about their hopes and dreams and expectations for the season was a truly inspiring experience. We ended the meeting with having everyone mention the thing they loved most about their team and then did 45 minutes of conditioning, because the best way I know to show your teammate how much you care is to have her watch you bust your tail in team conditioning. That night, I remember telling my assistant coach that if we were going to win a championship that year, it would be because of that meeting. As it turned out, I was right.

Communicating with, not at your team

Meetings like this don't always work and you may have to guide them more than I had to with this particular group of women that particular year. But the bottom line is that I believe coaches should always be straight up with their players and, to the extent possible, include them in the process. Tuckman suggested that teams that make it out of the storming phase almost always have participative leaders.

And besides, our players are way too good at seeing right through us if we attempt to make them buy in by circumventing the truth. They much prefer to see us honest (and, sometimes, vulnerable). This approach both creates and requires a high level of trust between coach and team. The good news is, that this is no chicken and the egg dilemma; it is actually pretty clear which comes first. I believe that the solution begins with openness and honesty, which in turn creates the trust that you need to make it work. There is no substitute for sincerity.

When I had to dismiss our team captain from the team for shoplifting, only two weeks before our conference championships, my team needed to know how much I cared for the individual that had made the poor decision, but that I had to do what was right for the team and let her go. We chose to explicitly address the issue in a team huddle. I explained the steps we were taking to ensure the player stayed in school and finished her degree, and we talked about how we could support her even though she was no longer on the team. Even though the player understandably had no desire to talk to me directly for a while, behind the scenes I stayed in touch with professors and mentors and through her teammates we made sure that she remained connected with the school and ultimately got her degree. That particular storming phase had a good ending because the team and coaches realized everyone was working toward the same goal. Two weeks later, we won our first conference championship.

Communication and Team Building

Team building is the process of a team coming together in pursuit of a common goal. Tuckman's model shows that there are stages that teams go through in coming together towards performance, and most teams need guidance as they go through these stages. It is the task of the coaching staff to build a team that traverses through the first three stages and ultimately ends up in the "performing" stage. The team building process is a very complicated one. I find it ironic that "*team building*" has sometimes gotten a bad reputation. Most people associate it with intervention techniques and sport psychology consultants.

You see, all over the world, any time a team is in trouble or performance is lacking in any way, sport psychologists are called in to help and they call it team building. It has helped create the image that a sport psychologist is the last resort when the coaching staff is at their wits' end. This image usually involves a team going to a high ropes course (the magical cure-all), or talking through their deepest fears and innermost secrets in long team meetings.

The truth is that team building is nothing like this preconceived notion, and you'd be amazed how many sport psychologists have never actually been on a high ropes course. I believe that coaches should use the option of outside intervention very carefully. If used sparingly and under the right circumstances, it can be a very powerful tool. But as soon as it's perceived as the "quick fix", it loses all credibility. The most effective team building takes places before problems arise. When the team is in trouble, even a sport psychologist doesn't have an easy solution. After all, even the best captain can't steer a ship that has no rudder.

In the early stages of the development of my program at Clarkson, we would bring in a performance consultant on a regular basis. We did the high ropes course, and we did the quintessential "mine field" and "toxic waste" exercises, along with many more. These are all great things to do with teams for many reasons. If you've never been on a high ropes course before, it's highly entertaining to watch teammates deal with their fear of height. However, it is of course twice as much fun to watch your coaches deal with it.

Mostly, these activities are fun and break the routine of on court training. Sometimes teams really appreciate a day off doing something different than playing volleyball. But you could achieve that same objective by having them play a spirited game of kick ball in practice. Or, if you happen to be Dutch like me, you could introduce the baffling game of "korfball" (Youtube it!) to your team. Be sure to require them to use the "reverse 6" shooting technique. Success guaranteed! The point is that you don't need a sport psychologist for this.

We've also brought in the same consultant to lead team conversations. At times, we noticed tensions were high and things needed to be talked through as a team. Rather than leading the discussions as coaches, we thought it would help to have an objective outsider some in and help get to the heart of the problems. One time, we struggled with some homesickness, and on another occasion, there was a conflict between two players that had started affecting our on court performance. Many a team sobbing session later, I now have a different opinion. Whenever possible, and unless the topic of conversation involves the coaches themselves, I think it's important that the team learns to trust the coaching staff in the process of venting issues or approaching delicate topics. While some players liked the objectivity of an outsider when discussing issues as a team, the majority of them would tell us afterwards that they had wished things could've stayed within the team.

What makes the activities lead by a consultant unique is their expertise in post-activity breakdown and feedback. A true team building activity involves some sort of evaluation at the end during which the point is explained and the team gets a chance to talk about their experience. It can be helpful to have a professional who's trained in doing this help the team, especially if you're trying to establish norms and values and are in teaching mode. Even though here, too, coaches can do a lot themselves. Don't get me wrong: I have a degree in sport psychology and in no way am I trying to convince you that the use of sport psychologists is overrated. I'm merely trying to argue that sport psychology consultants are misused. Many coaches substitute a consultant's intervention for great communication and guidance that should be coming from the coaching staff.

In my opinion, the most vulnerable area in team building is not the interaction between the players, but the connection between coaching staff and players. Depending on the kind of season you're having, or the types of players that are on the team, this area can be under some pressure. It is important for successful communication that there is a level of trust and a mutual understanding of viewpoints. But that's not always the case. It is in this area that my most successful experience with an outside consultant took place. During the 2009 season, our first championship season, we brought in a former Division I coach, who is now a performance consultant. She specializes in the use of the so-called DISC-behavioral model. The foundation for the DISC model comes from the work of a Harvard psychologist named Dr. William Moulton Marston in the 1920s. His theory was that people tend to develop a self-concept based on one of four factors — Dominance, Inducement, Steadiness, or Compliance (DISC).

Dr. Marston's theory goes on to link certain behavioral traits to the different factors. Depending on your classification, your response to stress is different from people with a different classification, for example. And so is your preferred way of communicating, or your study habits and skills. We had everyone on my team (including the coaches) take the DISC assessment tool, and then talked the team through all the individual idiosyncrasies. For example, it helped my players see why certain people are talkative on the bus after a tough loss, while others just want to be left alone. It may not be that the talkers care less; they just deal with stress and grief differently.

We found it incredibly helpful in helping players understand their teammates' (and coaches') different reactions to different situations. And ultimately, it helped them understand how they could best approach each other and me if they had an issue. I respond better to facts and solutions than to emotions, for example. My players now know to come into my office with a plan and with concrete questions.

If team development and team building is the engine that drives a successful season, communication is the motor oil that facilitates the process. Coaches are ultimately responsible for the quality of the communication but it can be helpful to bring in advice from the outside if it means facilitating a better understanding between coaches and players. Outside consultants should never be a substitute for old-fashioned coach-player interaction, however.

3

Confidence Building and Goal Setting

We had won only a hand full of matches until the final weekend, that first season at Clarkson. For all intents and purposes we were down for the count and dragging our sorry butts to the finish line of the season. It had been one of those years that would be enough for any coach to throw in the towel as it was. But we had one more weekend left to go, our conference tournament. I had walked to the back of the bus to talk to my team about our goals going into this final weekend of play. We would play the other four teams in the tournament in a round-robin setup and our first match of the day was against Skidmore College, the host team favored to win the championship. I vividly remember this moment, because of how stunned I was with the response from my team. I asked them what they expected from the match and they didn't hesitate with their answer. Here they were, this bunch of beat up, wrung out, exhausted players, but they were convinced: "*We are going to win it all and start by putting Skidmore in their place*". I remember being completely baffled. "*Put them in their place?*" Were they serious? It seemed to me that we were the little ants warning the big elephant to step aside or we would trample him. While on the one hand, I couldn't understand where this source of (false) confidence came from, on the other hand I had to be in awe of my team's ability to be that optimistic and confident. To be sure, Skidmore wasn't quite willing to cooperate that night. We didn't have a snowball's chance in hell to win that match and lost in three brutally short sets, but I have since done a lot of thinking about the power of confidence and goal setting.

Sources and Levels of Volleyball Confidence

Many (if not all) volleyball coaches would probably tell us that "momentum" plays a huge role in our sport. This is not necessarily an obvious statement, because research in the area of sport psychology has actually mostly failed to prove its existence.

But if you've ever been on the losing end of a 13-15 set, where you had been up 13-7 going into a time-out, you probably feel like you know better. I am certainly a believer. I often feel like I'm walking a tight rope in the balancing act of keeping my team focused on the present and the positives, while coaching them on what needs to be improved. It's a delicate process. Wresting momentum back from a team, or keeping it going at the right time, are difficult concepts. I'm convinced that a lot of it has to do with confidence. And unfortunately confidence is by nature almost as elusive as momentum.

Volleyball is a game of errors. In a situation where your team wins a set 25-23, you still give up 23 points - all likely errors of some sort (aces, missed digs, swings, etc.). Volleyball play have to deal with the realization that no matter how well they play, they are still going to give up points due to errors - a ton of them. Because we'd like to be able to count on our players from point to point, a relatively stable form of confidence is crucial. Think about the perfectionists on your team who dwell on their mistakes while the next point is already underway. Inevitably this leads to more mistakes and a snowball effect. Most players get stuck playing "the last ball" instead of focusing on "the next ball" (which is of course the most important ball).

I'm a beginning golfer so there are unfortunately many differences between Phil Mickelson's game and mine. But none are more glaring than Phil's ability to recover from a bad shot. You see, even Master's Champions occasionally hit a bunker or shank a drive. The championship isn't lost on one bad shot, it's won on the next one. When I end up in a bunker, the entire hole usually turns into a disaster on the scorecard. Great champions are masters at not letting the entire hole turn into a triple-bogey but following a bad shot with a great one. I have yet to learn that lesson on the golf course, unfortunately. But I've learned it on the volleyball court.

A positive explanatory style is a must for a volleyball player in order to maintain a solid level of confidence. Actually, the importance of a positive explanatory style has far reaching consequences. It has been shown that starters on collegiate teams have significantly higher levels of confidence than substitutes[3].

---

3   This is only true if the substitutes feel they should be subs. If subs think they should be starters, their confidence is no different from the actual starters.

Purpose

ue as well: the higher an athlete's confidence, at she is a starter.[4] If you can get over a mistake it away in a way that allows your confidence to stay high, your ⎯ ds of being a contributor on your team appear to be higher.

The constant ongoing dilemma that volleyball coaches face is, of course, how to increase their players' confidence level to allow them to handle the pressures of the error-filled game and to perform optimally.

Researchers at Miami University of Ohio, led by Dr. Robin Vealey, have identified nine sources of sport confidence[5]. According to a thesis done at the University of Minnesota, it turns out that female collegiate volleyball players have a preference of which sources they use for their confidence. They are listed below in that order of preference:

Sources of Volleyball Confidence

1. Social Support — Includes an athlete's support network; significant others, family and coaches

---

4   Dulfer, J. (2003). Sources and levels of trait sport-confidence among female collegiate volleyball players. (Unpublished master's thesis). University of Minnesota, Minneapolis, MN.

5   Vealey, R.S. (2001). *Understanding and enhancing self-confidence in athletes.* In R.N. Singer, H.A. Hausenblas, & C.M. Janelle (Eds.). Handbook of sport psychology (2nd ed., pp.550-565). New York: John Wiley & Sons.

2. Mastery — Derived from improving skills or becoming proficient in a skill

3. Physical/Mental Preparation — Is a source of confidence to those who are mentally/physically ready to perform

4. Coaches' Leadership — An athlete's perception of his/her coach being able to make good decisions and be a good leader

5. Demonstration of Ability — Becomes a source of confidence when athletes can show off their learned skills

6. Vicarious Experience — Watching peers (such as teammates or friends) perform successfully

7. Environmental Comfort — Feeling comfortable in surroundings such as the gym

8. Physical Self-Representation — The way in which an athlete perceives his/her physical appearance

9. Situational Favorableness — An athlete's perception of certain breaks going in his/her favor (example: momentum)

As coaches, it would be helpful to know which sources we should focus on to get our athletes to experience the highest levels of confidence. The good news for us is that three of these sources are actually significant predictors of our athletes' levels of confidence: physical/mental preparation, vicarious experience and situational favorableness.

It turns out that both physical/mental preparation and vicarious experience are positive predictors. This means that the more athletes rely on these sources, the higher their confidence is. It makes sense of course: If we teach our athletes to rely on being mentally and physically ready, we are teaching them to rely on something we control. This is also why I hammer on the concept of embracing the elephant in the room in terms of being mentally prepared. We cannot be prepared if we choose to ignore the pressures and stress that come with intense situations. The third source is a negative correlation: The more our athletes rely on situational favorableness, the *lower* their confidence is. This also makes sense; the last thing we want is for our athletes to rely on something they do not control (a referee's call, or an opponent serving two aces off the top of the net and starting a run). The factor of control is crucial in creating a stable level of confidence.

I suggest doing this little exercise with your team. Draw a circle on a white board and ask your team to name things about the game they can control. The controllables go in the circle – the circle of control. They'll come up with things like "how hard we work", "sleep", "serving" and a few other things they have complete control over. Then, have them name things they can't control: the uncontrollables. These go outside the circle, all the way around. Here, they'll list things like "officials", "bus rides", "lighting in the gym", "how tall their block is", "size of the crowd" and "opponent's attitude". It is amazing how many more uncontrollables your team can probably name versus things they have control over. There are many more and it is easy to get distracted and spend the majority of our energy worrying about the things that –per definition- we cannot control. It is a coach's task to create an environment that teaches athletes to "*control the controllables.*"

Goal Setting

The key to understanding goals is tied in with understanding your players better. Unfortunately, we can't set a goal for a team and just hope that everyone buys in. They might, but the odds of this happening are about the same as the odds of everyone on your team liking the same food. Everyone is different and responds to various goals differently. Some of my players are ultimately driven by "outcome" goals. These players tend to judge their performance on wins and losses. Oftentimes, players like this are what's called "ego-oriented". Other players are more focused on so-called "process" and "performance" goals. These players are more "task-oriented". It is a mistake to treat them all the same and as coaches we have to work hard to teach ego-oriented players to handle (and maybe appreciate) process and performance goals and to teach task-oriented players to work with outcome goals. I'm convinced my team needs a blend of both to be successful.

So what do we need to keep in mind as we're setting our process and outcome goals? You've probably heard the acronym "S.M.A.R.T" for goal setting. The letters represent the following:

S   Specific
M   Measurable
A   Attainable
R   Relevant
T   Time-Bound

Specific Goals

Specificity of goals refers to setting goals that athletes can wrap their heads around. If you're like me, you have probably sat down at the beginning of your season, while looking at your schedule, and you've tried to figure out how many matches you might win that season. I personally really like that exercise, but it cannot turn into a goal setting moment for my team, because winning a certain number of matches is not specific enough. It depends on too many factors that may not be within our control.

Measurable Goals

We are lucky (or cursed) that in our sport, virtually every contact is graded, and measured. We call them "statistics" and it's almost impossible to escape them. But for goal setting purposes, they actually can come in very handy. In the example below, the statements at the bottom are examples of measurable goals. Every couple of years, I do a little exercise just like that to see how we compare to the teams at the level that we're trying to get to.

Goal Setting Exercise Using Statistics

Statistical Comparison 2012 Season

	KPS	K%	E%	Hit%	Assist/S	Ace/S	EPS	DPS
Salisbury	13.17	.374	.125	.248	11.70	2.13	1.10	16.69
Elmhurst	13.10	.366	.126	.240	12.10	1.60	1.40	16.40
Calvin	13.50	.392	.122	.270	12.70	1.50	1.74	15.30
Puget Snd	13.08	.316	.131	.185	12.14	1.87	1.57	21.10
UMASSB	11.50	.340	.147	.193	10.40	1.90	1.78	15.50
CNU	13.80	.395	.117	.278	12.50	1.80	2.08	16.70
Hope	13.90	.389	.121	.268	12.80	2.00	1.83	17.00
Clarkson	**13.15**	**.360**	**.136**	**.225**	**11.67**	**2.39**	**2.28**	**16.20**

1. We are right on par in kills per set (KPS) with the top teams in the country
2. Our Hitting Percentage is a little on the low side because we make too many errors compared to the top teams
3. If for every 10 balls hit, we can change one "attempt" into a "kill" or one "error" into an "attempt", we would be right on track.
4. Our Aces/Set ratio is excellent, even though our errors are on the higher side. This is in line with our philosophy

(Challenging yet) Attainable Goals

If our goal is to have our athletes feel like they control their efforts and destiny, then we have to make sure to set appropriate goals. This is where many of us struggle. My first year at Clarkson, I had very little understanding of the level of competition we would face and what it would take for a team to be successful in our league and our region. The result was that we went in blind. My eternally optimistic team had decided they were going to beat everyone, no matter how unrealistic that was, and I was their biggest fan, who failed to channel their efforts appropriately. We lost. A lot. And yet, their goal was to win our championship (which no Clarkson team had ever done at that time). Even after realizing our predicament for that season, I neglected to adjust our goals, allowing my team to keep dreaming. In retrospect, that was a recipe for failure.

I'm absolutely convinced that many coaches struggle with the balance between realistic goals and challenging goals, just like I did that year. It is very important to let your team dream. But when your team is going to be struggling to make the conference tournament, a goal to "win a national championship", for example, only leads to feelings of failure and lower confidence, diminished effort and ultimately poor performance.

Relevant Goals

It goes without saying that your players have to buy into the goals that they're trying to accomplish. You probably have no problems trying to get them revved up for a matchup with your crosstown rivals, or for the championship match in the conference tournament. But can you make them see the importance of a mid-week matchup against the number last in the conference? Creative goal setting might come into play here.

Time-Bound Goals

The last general quality of a well-set goal is that it's time-bound. I prefer sitting down with my athletes and working on strength and conditioning goals that state they will get their vertical up to 23 inches by the end of a certain segment of our season, rather than just stating I want their vertical up. It makes the goal tangible and real for them to know a time line.

Team Involvement

As it turns out, it actually matters how you arrive at your team goals. As coaches, we have much more time to think about the future of our program than our athletes do. Between classes, their social lives and homework, it's safe to assume our players have a lot more on their minds than just volleyball and that means that we as coaches probably stress more about our program's goals than our athletes do.

Every year at the start of preseason, I remind my team what our program goals are. This is non-negotiable, and the standard by which we judge ourselves. It is why they bought in and signed on to play for me in the first place. But from there, I feel there has to be open dialogue with my players about two things: 1) the goals they have for the team for that season as we strive for our program goals, and 2) their individual goals. I strongly believe that my team has to be involved in this process.

Research has shown that those players who feel they don't have a strong grasp on their environment (external locus of control), prefer coach-set goals, while athletes who have an internal locus of control, prefer to set their own goals. It is important to include a mix of both, and also set both process and performance as well as outcome goals.

I know of a very successful Division I women's soccer team that employed the following strategy for their goal setting. Their overall goal was to finish top-4 in the Big Ten. To do that, the team had identified statistical categories that had to be improved upon. The categories included "shots", "shots on goal" and "possession time", I believe. There were probably more, and they were all objectively measurable. The team then showed its artsy side by creating a huge mural of a mountain in their locker room. It was a symbol of the mountain they were going to climb and the mountain had a path zigzagging to the summit. After each game, the coaches would inform the team about whether or not they had achieved their selected statistical goals. For each goal attained, they earned a sticker of a footprint that they attached to the mural. If they also won the game, their footprints doubled. For each number of footprints that made their way up the mountain, there were prizes along the way. At 25, they earned the right to design their own practice. At 50, they received a day off, and at 75, their coaches had to shave their heads. 100 footprints got them to the summit and had been calculated to be enough to accomplish their goal. I don't remember exactly what the incentives were, but the team was excited about it and had voted and agreed on it together before starting the project. They had all bought in. It's an excellent example of a goal setting strategy that utilized both coach-set and athlete-set goals, and included both process and outcome goals.

4

Building a Support Structure

A new season brings new possibilities. Dreaming about those possibilities is one of the best things about coaching. Well before a season even starts, the excitement builds as lineups play through my head and drills make it into my notebook. It helps if you are particularly excited about the talent coming back, but even if you're not sure about the level of talent, the excitement of starting with a blank slate should be ever-present. Dr. Tom Martin, the very successful head men's soccer coach at James Madison University, once told me that he believes when those moments of fun and anticipation are no longer present, no matter what kind of team you have coming back, it's finally time to get out of coaching. I think he's right.

But the truth is, that whether or not you'll have a successful season is not entirely in your hands. Nor is it completely determined by the players you have coming back. And it certainly doesn't start at the beginning of a season. It depends on all the things I've talked about. It depends on your mindset, communication, your success in team building, and on your goals. It depends on whether or not our team can come out of the storming stage and on so much more. But the question of whether or not your teams will ever even be in a position to compete for success is, in my opinion, answered in a much earlier stage. It coincides with the question: Who is in your corner? This is a question that we can control to some extent. Without the proper foundation, no matter how beautiful the house, it'll crumble in a storm. As you build your program, as much purpose should be directed towards a team's external relationships as towards the team and the game itself.

Let me explain what I mean by that. A team has many supporters and fans. From the parents and the fans who come to games, to you as their coach, to everyone who liked you on Facebook.

But it doesn't stop there of course. A team's support base has to be much broader for it to succeed. I'm willing to argue that the most important supporters of a team have to be your athletic directors, your department secretary, your equipment manager, your custodial staff, your president, and your dean of admissions and their staff. Without any of those groups, it's going to be very hard to succeed, or to have any kind of lasting success.

Commitment to an Open Mind

I remember having my doubts about taking the job at Clarkson during the interview process. For all the reasons I mentioned earlier, it wasn't a foregone conclusion that a volleyball program at Clarkson could ever have the kind of success I was envisioning.

But one thing stood out that alleviated a lot of my doubts: the commitment the administration was making, not only to the success of its sports, but also to the success of its coaches. From talking to other coaches and interacting with the athletic directors on my campus visit, I learned that the coaching staff was a very close-knit group with a lot of support from the higher-ups, which included the university president.

Of course, I didn't make it easy for them to believe I was the right person for the job when I asked the athletic director if I would be allowed to fly in recruits. She looked at me with this weird look in her eyes and answered "*umm...sure...so long as your recruiting budget can cover that*". What she was really thinking was that since my recruiting budget only had about $1400 in it and the nearest airport is 2.5 hours away, I was going to be disappointed pretty quickly. But I was only interested in hearing her support the idea of doing something that hadn't been done before (and is not very often done in Division III at all). I figured if we'd do it, we'd work on the pesky details of how to afford it later. It's important for those in charge to commit to keeping an open mind.

I am also blessed to work for people who from day one have chosen to stay the course, no matter what storms entered our path. On my end, I have always let them know what issues I expected. Just as I write up little expectations and predictions for my recruits, I do so for my boss as well. The first few years especially, I would make sure I kept my AD posted on possible outcomes of decisions I was contemplating regarding cutting players, or disciplinary action I was taking. I was making sure nothing would come as a surprise and they wouldn't be caught off guard if parent phone calls would come in early in the morning or if disgruntled players requested meetings with them behind my back. Most athletic directors and college presidents want their volleyball programs to increase their success, but I'm convinced that not all of them would probably be too excited about the potential turmoil that can cause in the initial stages of building the program. Can we really blame them? It takes a lot of purpose to turn onto the highway of change, and it requires even more purpose to stay on that highway until your final destination and not taking the first possible exit to safety.

Sometimes the only way out of hell is through it

Unfortunately, the turmoil is almost inevitable when you're building a program. It's actually the sign of progress and it's imperative to keep that in mind at all times. People have asked me what the pivotal moment was in the complete turnaround of our program and that's a very difficult question to answer. I think the answer is twofold.

First, I was lucky to find players willing to go on the journey with me, who cared as much as I did, and sometimes even at the expense of their own playing time. And second, I always received support at every turn during the years where our very progress caused the very issues that were actually a sign that we were on the right track.

For years, almost every single player who made it through four years in the program eventually saw their playing time diminish as they aged through the program. This is of course a normal progression if you're going to get better. Each recruiting class brings better players into the program, which can be a scary and threatening development for the current players. You could be undisputed starter one year and be spending a lot of time on the bench the next year. While it may have been disappointing for some of them at times, I am blessed that years after their graduation, many of the alumni still take great pride in the program and stay in touch on a regular basis. Even those who may have had their roles reduced or changed during their tenure on the team. This is a testament to their ability to commit to a goal that was greater than any individual.

I think it helped that from day one, I have always referred to our goals as "*our project*". I really feel that way. I might be the one in charge, but the program is only as good as they want it to be. Even when we were a not-so-good team in 2006, we talked about what we wanted to accomplish and started acting like the champions we would ultimately become. If we lost a big match, we would talk about what we needed to do to start winning matches like that down the road. If we saw a good team perform, we would discuss how we could get to that level. Sometimes it was almost like my players were my assistant coaches in a way - helping me map out how to get our team to the next level.

In 2007, at the start of my second season, I decided to test my new group of players. During our first meeting of the year I explained to the team, which consisted mostly of new recruits, that our first program goal would be to finish with a winning record. Going from 7-25 in our first year to a winning record would surely be a major milestone in our development. I also told them that it would be quite the accomplishment if we managed to do it in two seasons. With our youth and inexperience, I said that I expected us to start winning more at the end of their sophomore years. They were quiet during the meeting, but it took no more than 24 hours before the five freshmen requested a meeting with me and came to my office.

I had insulted them, they said. If our goal was to have a winning record, they wanted to do it *this* year, not next year. I remember having a hard time not smiling too much when they were in my office. They were obviously upset with me and I didn't want to insult them and their concerns, but I was just so happy with their mind set. After the meeting, I remember thinking to myself I had recruited the right players as I adjusted our goal for the year in my head. We ended up going 23-17 on the season, a winning percentage of .575. It was one of the biggest single season turnarounds in the NCAA that year.

The second reason for our program's turnaround has a lot to do with the first one. Once you bring in players with the right mindset, you need the support from the top that will ensure stability during the development of the program. Not everyone is able or willing to come along for the journey, and not everyone is going to be okay with their changing roles in the program. In our case, we lost one or two players every year, and we even had to part ways with an assistant coach. I am 100 percent convinced that our willingness to go through these difficult times, and the support and encouragement we received to do it, enabled us to turn the corner as quickly as we did. At several points along the way, my supervisors made it absolutely clear to everyone that they supported the road we had chosen and let me know they had my back, no matter how ugly things would get. Sometimes it was just a quick pick-me-up meeting with me, and sometimes it was meeting with my players to point out that playing collegiate volleyball is a privilege and not a right. No matter how it happened, it was always very clear the support was in place and everyone was a united front. Sometimes the only way out of hell is through it. It may not be a journey that's always fun, but it sure makes for a great story afterwards.

In my e-mail account, I have a folder where I keep all the negative feedback that mostly originated during those difficult years. It reminds me of how far we've come and how important it is to keep looking ahead and progressing. From time to time I browse the e-mails. It's the best motivation I can think of. And for all those nasty e-mails and complaints there is one to offset them in another e-mail folder, where I keep the positive comments. When you get to that make or break point where you're not sure you want to continue the journey through hell, take a look at how many positives there are in that particular folder. I think it'll make you want to go forward. One of my favorite things about my job is staying in touch with our alumni and to realize how proud they are of where the program is now.

Vince Lombardi once said that he believed that any man's finest hour, the greatest fulfillment of all that he holds dear, is that moment when he has worked his heart out in a good cause, and lies exhausted on the field of battle –victorious. I believe that perhaps the only thing better than that is the moment where you look around and realize your teammates are right there, next to you.

Building the Support

So the lesson is that as much time as we spend within our team fabric, that's how much effort needs to be devoted on developing those external relations. If you're lucky, like me, this is a fun part of the job and it doesn't necessarily require extra effort. I really enjoy talking to our department secretary about the progress the team has made over the years. She's been to many home games and even more away games over the years, so she would know.

And our dean of admissions has brought his kids to our games and meets with many of my recruits, so he has a personal connection to a lot of my players. It makes it fun to keep him posted on developments in the program. Our president and his wife have come to many home games and "bribe" our team with a meal at their house if we have a good season. It's become one of our favorite team traditions. And my athletic director has learned more about volleyball in the past seven years than I think he wants to admit. I keep him in the loop as much as I can and we have had many discussions about my recruiting strategy that were very specific. He does this with all of the coaches in the department and while it may seem like micro-management at times,

I believe it's allowed him to keep a very accurate finger on the pulse of each program. I believe a program cannot exist without this involvement. It cannot exist without the cleaning lady leaving candy in the locker room as a thank you for a birthday card, and it cannot exist without my team knowing the president and his wife by name. Well that's a lie. It can exist, but it wouldn't be nearly as successful.

5

Tactical Choices within the Game

Once you decide on the brand of volleyball your team will embrace, it is time to decide how you will get really good at that particular brand. This chapter could be different for everyone, but for us they are the major things we focus on in our quest to play low error, high efficiency volleyball. Those elements define our style and became our trademark. They define our gym culture and our decision-making. In short: It's what we believe in.

A. Serving

The absolute cornerstone of my coaching philosophy is our serving mindset. At Clarkson, all of my players have a jump serve of some sort. Many did not come in with it, but all of them develop it early and are asked to use it and put as much speed on the ball as they can to be successful. More and more evidence exists that serving speed is beginning to affect the technique used by the passers. Because (for now) overhead passing is allowed, many passers are being taught to employ a backwards-moving technique where the passers start shallow and move back with the approaching ball. With increased serving velocity, this technique is going to ultimately cause problems when there simply isn't enough time to move back far enough, especially when a ball is too difficult to pass with the fingers. I like the fact that we can force the issue and stress passers by training our servers to put some extra sauce on their serves by jumping.

I cannot begin to describe how many spectators have expressed their concern about how many serving errors we sometimes make as a team. There are matches where the number is low, but there are of course also matches where the errors outnumber the aces - sometimes by quite a margin. Many of these observers, including many opposing coaches, will proceed to tell me that if we were to just stay standing, and put the ball in play, we would be much more successful. I've heard it all before. Sure, I could easily ask my players to tie a helium balloon to the ball and send it over the net. But would it really make us more successful? My response is that those who claim it would are simply dead wrong. In the 2012 NCAA national quarterfinals, we were up against a formidable opponent in soon-to-be national champions St. Thomas of Minnesota. In watching film, we had determined that from a pure talent viewpoint, we were the clear underdog. Their blockers were bigger, and their hitters stronger than ours.

But we noticed that their serving strategy was different than ours. Like many (if not most) elite teams, they seemed to want to rely on their blocking and their defense. It appeared that they were less willing to take risks on serve, instead wanting to put the ball in play in hopes to live to fight another day. I have noticed that as teams get better, their aggressiveness in the area of serving usually goes down a little bit. This is true across most levels.

In the spring of 2013, we scrimmaged a Division I team that had made the NCAA tournament that season and we had the same result. Our serving ability and strategy took them by surprise and made them quite uncomfortable. The score ended up way closer than it should've been based on an evaluation of talent alone. They were taller, jumped higher and hit harder. But they were so out of system that we hung with them and only lost by two points in all three of the sets.

So we decided to surprise St. Thomas and do the opposite of what good teams often do – we served as aggressively as we had all season long anticipating that it would catch them off guard. That was exactly what happened. We were much more in the match than you would expect based on talent alone. Our opponents spent the majority of the match attacking out of system and having to deal with uncomfortable situations, something they clearly weren't used to. If you don't like your chances and matchups given perfect circumstances, you have to change the game on your opponents. And the key to doing this is almost always serving.

With our stat taking and the use of a radar gun in our practices, our servers know what the speed is that will make them successful the majority of the time and they attempt to execute *every* time. I've read that the ace to error ratio has to be kept at a certain level, but my philosophy is that aces don't tell the whole story. If our serving game disrupts the opponent to the extent that they're out of system for the majority of the game, we can accept giving them a good number of "free points" (missed serves).

They say the serving game is the only part of the game you have complete control over. This of course holds true for the execution of the serve, but certainly not for the outcome. That depends on what happens on the other side of the net. In the world of statistics, most systems rate serves on a scale from 0-4, with 0 being an error and a 4 being an ace (a 0-pass by the opponent). A 3-serve would then equate to a 1-pass by the opponent. A 2-serve is a 2-pass and a 1-serve is the equivalent of a 3-pass. But those ratings depend on the ability of the passers on the other side of the net. In other words: A great serve against one opponent might not be so good against another opponent. On the one hand this is the fun part about a serving strategy: finding a target and serving strategically to that zone or person - finding the weakness in an opponent's passing lineup and taking advantage of it. But on the other hand it symbolizes a weakness in how we think about evaluating serves. The criteria change depending on who's on the other side of the net – a factor the server has no control over. And think about how this relates to how we train serving. If a terrible serve could potentially turn into an ace and a great serve could be passed right to target; how do we really define "terrible" and "great"?

Motor learning generally uses two extrinsic feedback mechanisms[6]. One is the so—called "knowledge of performance (KP)". This type of feedback deals with things like "was my shoulder high enough", "was the correct foot forward", and "was my toss high enough". The other type of feedback is the "knowledge of results (KR)" KR deals with the outcome of the action (in this case, the serve). Was it in or out? Was it to the correct zone, and was it fast enough? Because both types of feedback are crucial to performing a successful serve, it would make sense to look at whether or not they are both sufficiently present in our drills. Many serving drills consist of partners serving back and forth, or "mindless" serving into an empty court. In the learning stages of a movement, when you haven't mastered the skill yet, this can be very helpful. Coaches walk around and correct the serve, while tweaking little things.

However, when you're getting ready for competition and assuming mastery of the serve, doesn't it make sense to also have accurate knowledge of results? And if those results (the passing accuracy of the opponent) are subjective, doesn't it make sense to come up with a way to make them a little bit more objective? As it turns out, the result of your serve might be correlated to its speed. And speed is measurable.

While working on my graduate degree at the University of Minnesota in the fall of 2001, I was fortunate to work with head coach Mike Hebert, the visionary hall of famer, who had seen

---

6   Magill, R.A. (2001). *Augmented feedback in motor skill acquisition*. In R.N. Singer, H.A. Hausenblas, & C.M. Janelle (Eds.). Handbook of sport psychology (2nd ed., pp.86-114). New York: John Wiley & Sons.

the results of incorporating a radar gun in volleyball practices with the USA Women's National Team.

Coach Hebert asked me to keep serving stats on all of his players throughout the season, and we kept track of the execution of the serve (float, jump or jump float) and two types of results: the resulting pass, and also the speed of the serve. After the halfway point of the season, we performed an analysis of the speed of the serves and related it to the pass quality. The outcome really helped the coaching staff coach the team's serving game in a way that wouldn't be possible without the aid of the radar gun. Each player received their own individual "serving profile", which showed which speeds were most successful for them. Some needed to hit the ball as hard as possible (this is generally true for topspin jump servers), while others were more successful hitting zones (and not worrying about speed). In general, we found that float serves and jump float serves were only successful at disrupting the opponents' offense at speeds above 42 mph. In the Big Ten, at that time, anything under that almost always resulted in an easy pass by the opponent.

The next step was to get out the radar gun in practice and give more detailed "knowledge of results" to the players. Rather than saying, "*serve faster*", or "*you are not putting enough pace on the ball*", we would have someone patrol the end line with a radar gun and give exact feedback. The players loved it and became extremely competitive with it. In fact, they liked it so much, that we ended up incorporating it into a promotions scheme during the home games. We would clock every serve with the radar gun and show the speed on the big screen. Anytime a serve exceeded 50mph we would throw T-shirts or mini volleyballs into the stands. It unleashed a fierce battle for the unofficial Gopher volleyball serving record.

At Clarkson, we unfortunately could not afford a radar gun. We briefly thought about asking the state police to set up shop in our gym, but as it turns out, the baseball coach was glad to help out and let us use his radar gun. Our practices have gone up in intensity and our goal of becoming the strongest serving team in the region is one step closer. During the 2011 and 2012 seasons we were consistently ranked in the top of Division III for aces per set, and our stats showed that our opponents were spending less time in system than they ever had before. At the upper level of Division III, it turns out that serve speeds of 38mph and upwards have the greatest chance of success. Before we go into any specific serving drills, we make sure that all of our servers know what their "record" is and we assign them a "bandwidth", which consists of their record minus 2mph (if my record is 40, my bandwidth is 38-40). When their record changes, we update it at the end of practice. For some, the bandwidth is not their record. The serving profile from our libero, for example, showed us that she is most effective serving around 39mph, while her record is 45mph. At that top speed, however, her error percentage is too high. Her bandwidth is 37-41 in practice, teaching her to be as aggressive as possible, while limiting her errors.

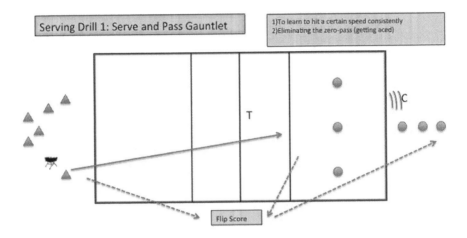

1. Divide the team into 2 groups: your primary passers ("passers") and everyone else ("challengers")
2. A coach patrols the opposite end line from the servers with a radar gun (C)
3. Each team gets 5 minutes to serve while the other team passes. Score is written down and then roles are reversed (do not keep a running score) – our games last 10 minutes
4. After each serve or pass, a player jogs to the flip score to adjust the score based on what they scored, before going back to the line

Assign every server a "bandwidth" of ± 2 of their fastest serve (unless a different speed is more effective for them). A +serve is a serve inside that bandwidth. A –serve is outside of the bandwidth or an error (to challenge the passers more, allow challengers two errors for every -2 points.) Bandwidths change after each practice.

Score:

Passers		Challengers
+1	3-pass	+2
+1	2-pass	+1
0	1-pass	+1
-2	0-pass	-1
+1	+ serve	+1
-2	- serve	-2

5. As a twist, I like playing the game as described and then asking both groups how they would like to change the scoring by one point so that it's more in their favor. Challengers might choose to make a 3-pass worth 3 points or they might make an error serve worth only -1 so they can serve tougher. Conversely, you can also give them the option to change the point worth for their opponents by plus or minus 1. My teams get really competitive with this.

Serving Drill 2: Red Rover | To learn what constitutes and aggressive serve and to associate that concept with speed

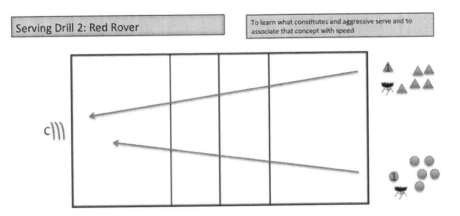

1. Divide the team into 2 groups and have them line up on the end line
2. A coach patrols the opposite end line with a radar gun
3. Both numbers one serve their best, most aggressive, serve which is measured by the coach with the radar gun
4. Both coaches vote (quickly) on whose serve was better (more aggressive) – a combination of speed and placement
5. The loser joins the winner's team. In case of a tie, both players stay
6. Play until one last player standing

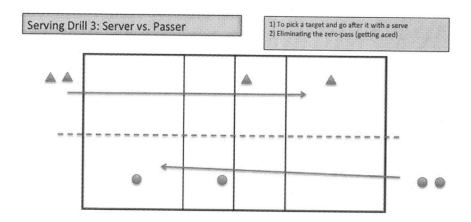

Serving Drill 3: Server vs. Passer

1) To pick a target and go after it with a serve
2) Eliminating the zero-pass (getting aced)

1. Servers are serving at one passer. Target judges the passes (0-3) and the passer's score. She starts at 0.

2. The passer's goal is to get to +3 for a big point. She gets a point for each 2-pass or 3-pass. 1-passes or aces are -1.

3. If the passer gets to +3, she gets a big point and starts at 0 again.

4. As soon as the passer gets below 0, she is out and becomes the target. Her place is taken by the server who's been a server the longest or who got her 'out'.

   Play for time (e.g. 5 minutes) and count big points.

5. This drill allows you to pit your best servers against your best passers and have them duke it out

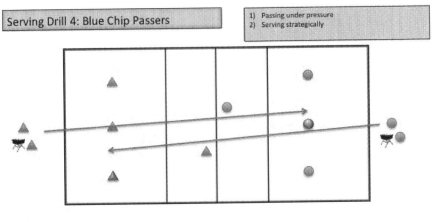

Serving Drill 4: Blue Chip Passers

1) Passing under pressure
2) Serving strategically

● ▲ Blue Chip Passers (pre-assigned)

1. Divide the team up into two groups. Each group has one "blue chip passer" in their midst. Change up this role every so often or assign it to your liberos.
2. Each team serves a number of serves (e.g. 25) – both sides alternate at a high pace
3. Blue chip passers earn extra points but also cost extra in case they make a mistake.
4. Consider playing to a certain score (e.g. 25)

Score:

Blue Chips		Teammates
+4	3-passes	+2
+1	2-passes	+1
0	1-passes	0
-4	Aces	-2

- Missed serves are -1 for the server's team

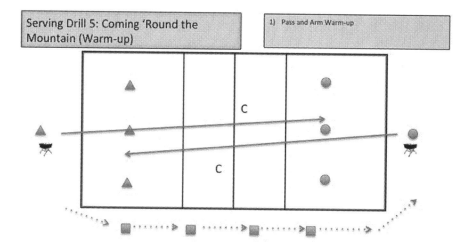

1. Team is divided into three groups
2. Two of the teams take the court, while the third team jogs around the court as ball retrievers.
3. Coaches are targets and score keepers
4. The goal is to get to 31 points first
5. Winner stays, losers become the jogging team

Score:

3-passes	+3
2-passes	+2
1-passes	+1
-Aces	-2

- Missed serves are -2 for the servers' team
- Tip: this is a great drill to start practice. Have servers throw the ball to their own team to start. It's a good arm warm-up and confidence builder.

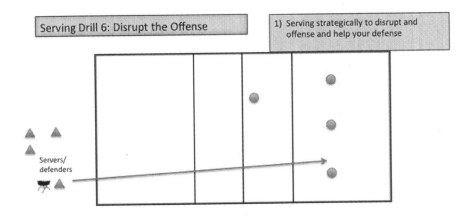

1. Team is divided into Servers and Attackers
2. Object of the game is the remain a server
3. Attackers convert an attack against an open court. If they convert (no tips), the server becomes a defender, making it harder to convert the next one. A dug ball is a wash and the server stays a server.
4. Once the fourth defender is added, both groups switch (i.e. attackers' goal is to convert 4 attacks)

Score: Consider playing 2-minute games, keeping your players aware of the time lapsed. At the end of the 2 minutes, those on the attacking side run a sprint.

B. Chaos Theory: The Out of System System

It is my firm belief that the key to victory in the game of volley-ball is to be as aggressive as possible, while keeping your error percentage as low as possible. Or, as I put it to my team: "*More purpose, less error*". It was the philosophy of the late Hans Geene, one of my Dutch mentors at the University of Groningen. He believed that the game was fundamentally very simple and had to be played that way. He would put us through the same drills, week in and week out and always talked about *"just reduce your errors"*. While I wholeheartedly agree with the underlying concept, I have added the concept of "purpose" to his philosophy so as not to have my players focus on the negative. Instead of asking them to reduce errors, I will remind them to have purpose. This could mean knowing what to do out of system or on a trap set, for example. In moments where errors are likely, I'm asking them to have a plan; a purpose. Attackers might be reminded to go "high, hard and deep" in those situations. Or they could go for an aggressive tip or wipe-off play. In essence, this is the "purple elephant" principle with reducing errors being the purple elephant. By asking you to focus on what to do (an aggressive play with purpose), rather than what *not* to do (making an error), I can hopefully accomplish two things at the same time – reducing errors, and creating an aggressive play.

It is of course impossible to cover all the aspects of the game so we have to make choices and prioritize. Over the course of a season, your team will spend a lot more time out of system than in system. We calculated during the 2012 season that in all our matches, on serve receive, we were only in system or approximately in system about 52% of the time. And that's just off a pass. If we add defense to the mix, your out of system percentage goes up dramatically.

It is safe to say that matches aren't won when everything is perfect. Teams that win matches are usually the teams that create order out of chaos, and that do best out of system, rather than in system.

The big lesson of this is that if you were going to spend a huge chunk of time out of system in matches, it would stand to reason you should practice this. For example, more and more teams are going away from traditional hitting lines. In our gym, you see less and less of it as well. It might make sense to have your setter warm up with you tossing balls to the 2/3 spot on the court to give her confidence. But the odds of her setting from that spot during the match are not great, so moving her around is important. The same applies to hitters. While swinging off a toss has its merits for reasons of confidence (and maybe to intimidate your opponent during a warm-up), ultimately how hard you can hit a perfect set against no blockers has very little to do with your chances of success hitting off a bad pass, from the three-meter line, against a double or triple block or with a less than perfect approach. How often have you seen a team look absolutely impressive in warm-up, only to wonder where that prowess went once the match started? When you add a pass and a block to the game, many teams look completely different. In my opinion it's because we haven't learned to be comfortable being uncomfortable.

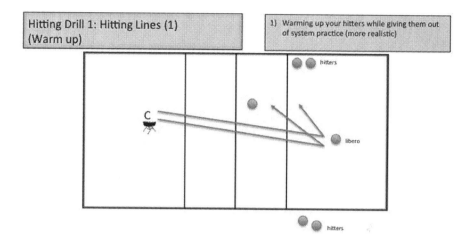

1. Coach enters down/free balls to the libero/passer.
2. The passer sends one ball the setter, and every other ball to the 10 foot line
3. Hitters hit two balls in a row before rotating to the back of the line

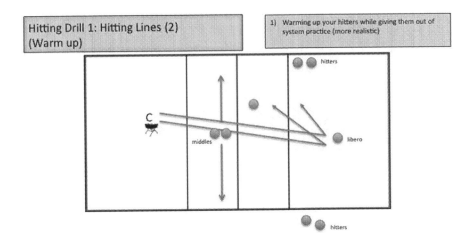

Hitting Drill 1: Hitting Lines (2) (Warm up)

1) Warming up your hitters while giving them out of system practice (more realistic)

1. Coach enters down/free balls to the libero/passer.
2. The passer sends one ball the setter, and every other ball to the 10 foot line
3. Hitters hit two balls in a row before rotating to the back of the line
4. Added: Middles start in MF, close on setter contact and stay and block both balls. Middles alternate sides.

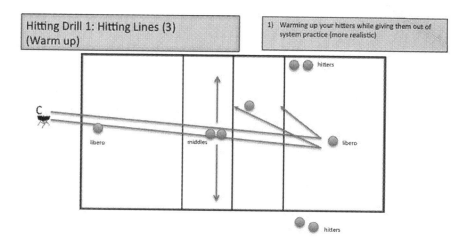

1. Coach (or libero) serves down/free balls to the libero/passer.
2. The passer sends one ball the setter, and every other ball to the 10 foot line
3. Hitters hit two balls in a row before rotating to the back of the line
4. Middles start in MF, close on setter contact and stay and block both balls. Middles alternate sides.
5. Added: libero starts in middle back and chooses a side upon or right after setter contact. It's the hitter's job to swing to the opposite (open) corner.

If your team is going to be better out of system than your opponent, I would argue that everyone on your team needs to be able to set a second ball intelligently. We spend a lot of time on this in practice, with feedback relating to both the technical component of a clean delivery, but also on decision-making skills and placement.

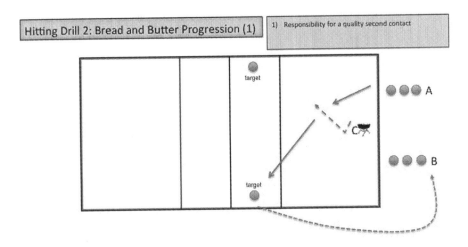

Hitting Drill 2: Bread and Butter Progression (1)

1) Responsibility for a quality second contact

1. Coach (C) bounces a ball off the floor into the middle of the court
2. Player from Line A steps in and sets the ball diagonally to target in zone 4, then becomes that target while the target goes to the end of line B
3. Player from Line B sets to zone 2 and target goes to line A
4. Count 20-30 good sets, far enough off the net and high enough to hit.

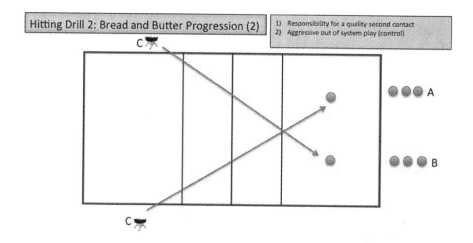

1. Coach 1 enters a ball to A who passes to B, and then attacks off of B's set. Hitters retrieve the ball and both A and B switch lines
2. Coach 2 enters the balls to B

Tip: Consider serving the ball from the end line for added passing practice

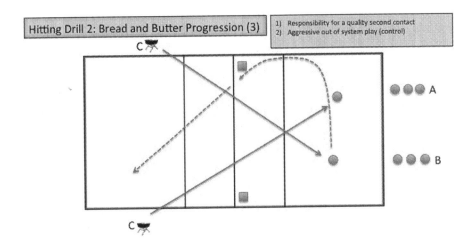

1. Coaches alternate and serve randomly to either line A or line B
2. Whoever does not receive the serve, sets the <u>opposite</u> attacker
3. Passer return to the back of the other line
4. Setter becomes the attacker, after covering
5. Attacker retrieves the ball and returns to the other line

Possible Goals:
- 25 good kills (coaches judgment)
- +25 good (errors are a minus)
- Keys: High, Hard and Deep

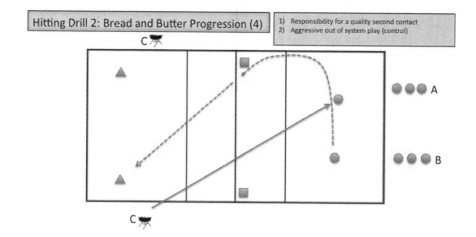

1. Coaches alternate and serve randomly to either line A or line B
2. Whoever does not receive the serve, sets the <u>opposite</u> attacker
3. Attacker attacks cross court to a defender
4. Passer return to the back of the other line
5. Setter becomes the attacker, after covering
6. Attacker becomes a defender
7. Defender retrieves the ball and returns to the back of the line

Possible Goals:

- 25 points (point is a kill (coaches judgment) OR defender dig and catch
- +25 good (errors are a minus)
- Keys: High, Hard and Deep

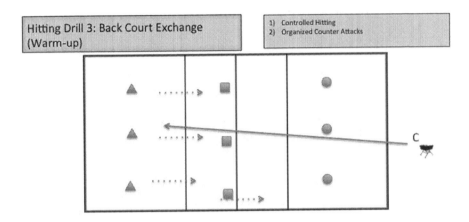

1. Team is divided into three groups
2. Two groups on, third group waiting by the net (not involved)
3. Ball is always entered to the side of 6
4. After the back row attack, the hitters become the waiting group, and the waiters take their place and so on and so forth
5. Tip: allow the waiting team to help on net balls to keep rally going

Goals:
- 8 in a row (beginning of the season)
- Work up to 25 good attacks in a row
- To heighten awareness, we add a "magic ball" in a different color. When this ball is entered, 20 wins the game.

Drill: Chaos: The art of the dirty street fighter

Have you ever coached them, the players who just seem to make things happen? Falling to their left, they pop a ball up with their right wrist, to have it land for a kill on the other side of the net. Or diving into the bleachers, they manage to keep a ball alive that you had already given up on. I'm talking about the tomahawkers and pancakers. My personal favorite is the defensive specialist who sends the first ball back over the net into a deep corner to score. Or what about the setter who turns around and pushes the ball into left back? In our gym, plays like that earn you the "dirty street fighter" badge of honor. Our players get excited about that term. One of the most popular games in our gym is "chaos", where we talk about scoring and finding ways to score, even when the usual ways to score aren't available (i.e. you're not allowed to jump and swing). We often stop the drill and talk about purpose. Are you just mindlessly hitting a down ball into the corner (which is super easy to defend), or do you actually try to make the opponent uncomfortable by pushing, tipping and aggressively attacking their weaknesses? I guess you could say the purpose of the game is to test the players' purpose. The game can last forever if both sides hit down balls, and it will turn into a great workout, but we'd be training the wrong thing if we allowed that. Ask your players to become dirty street fighters and watch your practices go to the next level in intensity and fun.

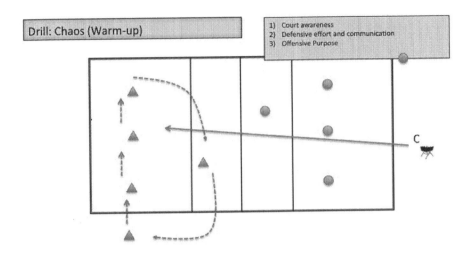

1. Team is divided into two groups
2. Three players on, additional players waiting in right (and/or left) back)
3. Rule: <u>NO JUMPING</u> when sending the ball over the net
4. After the ball is sent over, mandatory clockwise rotation (see arrows)

<u>Goals:</u> FIND WAYS TO SCORE
- We talk about "dirty street fighter mentality"
- Stop games to talk about open spots and strategies
- Down ball vs. pushed or tipped ball
- Communication
- Thinking: e.g. does "setter" need to block?
- Thinking: e.g. setting at the net on 3-meter line?

Coaching at a school with a heavy academic emphasis on the sciences has challenges, but in this case it also presents a nice opportunity. My players understand math and numbers very well. I have recently started talking to them about thinking about scoring points when they're sending the ball back over the net. The "scoring" works in a similar way as the Coleman system for passing stats.

Kill = 3 points
Forcing the other side out of system = 2 points
Keeping the other side in system = 0 points
Error = -1 point

Using this "system" allows me to give specific feedback. It helps remind our attackers that it's not necessary to go for the kill all the time (a 2 or 3 are both good results). And it also helps them understand why a simple down ball isn't a great option.

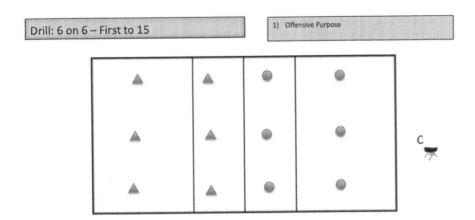

Drill: 6 on 6 – First to 15

1) Offensive Purpose

1. Team is divided into two groups
2. Teams are already switched into their rally positions.
3. We are only scoring the attack:
   kill = 3 points
   out of system = 2 points
   in system = 0 points
   error = -1 point
4. Balls are entered to alternate sides, unless one side got a kill, in which case they get the ball back.

Goals: FIND WAYS TO SCORE
- We talk about "dirty street fighter mentality"
- Stop games to talk about open spots and strategies
- Down ball vs. pushed or tipped ball
- Communication

C. Practice Intensity - Championship Points (Purpose Points)

Our philosophy is that aggressive, purposeful volleyball wins championships. I've spent years watching preseasons start out with lots of intensity and good resolutions. Pepper sessions are intense and bodies are flying all over the gym to dig balls that later on in the season end up dropping. If an impossible ball gets dug, but then not played by a teammate, or buried in the net by someone...eventually you run the risk that balls stop getting dug. Purpose has to be taught and instilled. But it also has to be relentlessly rewarded. At Clarkson we keep track of "purpose points" on the white board in the gym. Every time someone makes a championship effort on a play, they can be nominated (after the rally) by anyone, for a purpose point. If the coaching staff unanimously agrees, the point is awarded on the white board. But for every time a ball drops uncontested, or something happens that is not in line with how champions play, a point is added in the opposite column: the "obstacles". These points can result from lack of effort, missed assignments, or even eye rolling or communication problems. At the end of the week, we look at the balance of the points. We sprint for every obstacle point on the board, but the team is able to make up for it with their purpose points. If there are more of those than obstacle points, the sprints for the week are waved. Our conditioning consists of things other than running, which means that the team has full control over whether or not they run at all. For most players, this is a great incentive. Aside from the fact that it keeps everyone really keenly aware of the need for great effort and focus, you should see the energy in the gym when someone makes an unbelievable play. Hands will shoot in the air nominating someone's play and the cheers are loud when the coaches concur. Actually, the same happens during weekend tournaments. Sometimes the other team wonders what we are talking about when we nominate a play in the middle of a match, but championship effort just doesn't care what day of the week it is.

Idea to Reward Purpose: Ending practice or drills with an assignment

Sometimes the best way to get your team to show their competitive spirit in practice is to set a goal for them, through which they can end practice early. You may ask them to collect 35 kills, or 30 kill blocks, or get 30 good swings in a group pepper drill. We've all done this. But you may want to consider putting the entire onus on one player. It's the idea of getting them used to pressure all over again. I challenge you to ask your libero to dig 25 balls to end practice in the 6 on 6 drill, or maybe challenge your team to hit .250 as a team in a set to 25. There are lots of ways to get them to understand your point and to work their butts off to get out of the gym early.

Idea to Reward Purpose: The Pyramid Practice

Another way to utilize the competitive spirit of your team is to tell them practice is over when they accomplish all the drills you've designed. Make sure they all have objective goals and place them in order of easiest to hardest, as in a pyramid. Start with the easiest drill and if the team accomplishes the goal, move them to the next drill. Anytime they fail, you can move them back a step on the ladder, but as they accomplish the goal of the drill at the top of the pyramid, practice is over. Make sure that the thing you feel like you have to work the most on is in the middle of the pyramid (#3 or #4), as they will spend the most time on this. If your players are anything like mine, then my guess is you'll have a lot of fun with this, watching them compete.

Figure 4: Example of a Pyramid Practice

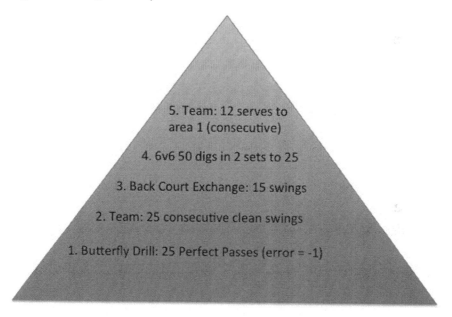

5. Team: 12 serves to area 1 (consecutive)

4. 6v6 50 digs in 2 sets to 25

3. Back Court Exchange: 15 swings

2. Team: 25 consecutive clean swings

1. Butterfly Drill: 25 Perfect Passes (error = -1)

D. In Match Coaching

Developing purpose on the court is a collaborative effort. As coaches, we try to instill and reward the right behavior. But the frustrating thing is that ultimately, on the court, when push comes to shove, it is up to your team to get the results. As a coach, alone on the sideline, you have much less control over the outcome than your setter and your outside hitter do. I believe that it is our job to be the calm supporters on the sideline. If my players aren't sure what to do, I want them to be able to look at me and see a calm and self-assured coach. You'll very rarely see me scream and yell (especially at officials).

I'm banking on the lessons that our practices have taught my players. It is very likely that I've asked my outside hitters a million times *why* they hit a certain shot. If they've gotten to the point where they could answer that question, then they just need me to be an ally in the heat of battle.

I can remind them what shots are open and what the other team's defense is doing to stop them, just incase they didn't see it. I don't need to yell at them (too much). I find myself coaching *with* my team, instead of coaching *to* them, most of the time. Don't get me wrong; there are a lot of time-outs where they get my wrath – particularly if the effort level isn't where it needs to be. But overall, what I tell them before most matches is also how I coach: *"Ladies, I look forward to battling with you out there tonight"*.

What I do is referred to as "coaching on the averages", but I like to refer to it as "coaching on the trends". It is our job as coaches to keep our eye on the big picture during matches. Are we executing our game plan? Is the game plan working or does it need adjusting? How is our energy and effort level? I believe that ultimately numbers don't lie. As long as you're putting in the effort and energy required, the team that makes the fewest errors while being more aggressive than their opponents will win the majority of the matches. This is the reason I am relatively calm on the bench. I see how some coaches coach their hardest when their team is neck and neck with the other team, but when the score isn't so close, they're nowhere to be found. It's a tough urge to resist: to sit back in disgust when our team is letting us down. But that's when they need us the most and that's when coaching is hardest. I remember losing the first set to a team from Buffalo 25-6 during the 2012 season. While I couldn't stem the tide that particular set, it was important to keep coaching and remind my team that eventually, we'd catch some breaks and they'd start to make a few more errors.

I find that simply reminding them of the trend that we're observing is sometimes all the coaching that's needed. *"Eventually, this is what's going to happen…"* is a great way to keep your team focused in a match. Against the team from Buffalo, that's exactly what happened and we won the next three sets pretty handily.

1. Time-outs

After we won our regional final match in 2012, Clarkson's men's lacrosse coach caught me in the hallway to offer his congratulations. But, he wondered, when we were up 24-21 in the second set and they scored three unanswered points, why on earth didn't I take a time-out? To be honest, until he asked me this very legitimate question, I hadn't even given it a second thought. He made a great point. We had ended up losing the set, and it would've made perfect sense to stop our opponents' momentum momentarily with a time-out. It's just that I had such confidence in my team that I didn't think they needed me to give them a break. Our passing wasn't the problem – we had struggled putting the ball away, but in my mind, that was just a matter of time. The next shot could be the kill to end it; why would I break *our* momentum?

Now, looking back, I think that our lacrosse coach might have made a better volleyball coach than me in that particular moment. But I think this possible minor hiccup was caused by my focus on the big picture. Coaches who are much smarter than I am have calculated that the team that arrives at 21 points first wins that set the majority of the time. This would imply that your time-outs, your coaching tools, would need to be used prior to this crucial moment in the set. But what if trust is a better tool than math? I am willing to believe that the majority of teams that get to 21 first go on to win, but that number includes a lot of blowout wins. If one team is clearly better than the other, they will almost always get to 21 first.

I'm much more interested in what happens in matches between evenly matched teams. It's not too strange to believe that in those matches, the most confident team, the team most able to deal with the pressure of a tight score, has the upper hand no matter what the score. And it is my firm belief that the biggest shot in the arm we can give our team is to keep our seat when everyone in the building expects a time-out. "*Coach must really trust us*".

Communication with your team in a time-out is not always easy. I've witnessed many coaches do it differently, and there may not be one right way to do it, but I'm convinced there are some ways how *not* to do it. For example, our inclination is often to point out to our players why they are playing poorly. Chances are, we've just lost a bunch of points and as coaches we feel like our team has abandoned us and is making us look silly. I see coaches take a time out and absolutely tear their team a new one. Ranting and raving for a minute can make you feel better, but I'm convinced that it ultimately doesn't help our team perform. They know they're losing and they're looking for a way out, a plan of action.

Communication needs to adhere to the same standards I talked about in chapter two: Communicate *with* your team (not *at* them), and make sure there's purpose in the conversation. I find it calming and reassuring to remind my players why things aren't going the way we want them to and then giving them a way to fix that. I usually look for ways to explain the reasons for us playing poorly through external factors. I might tell them that our opponents are playing better than they normally do and they'll come back down to earth soon as long as we hang in tough. Or I might say that our serving is not tough enough, allowing our opponents to run their offense. As soon as we go back to our "normal" serving game, I'll remind them, we will start seeing more success. Here, too, the positive explanatory style that confident players exhibit comes in very handy. And coaches can help their players a little using it.

Time-outs are generally considered great tools in the following circumstances:

1. To stop your opponent's momentum after a (string of) great play(s).
2. To (temporarily) silence a hostile crowd after your opponent did something great
3. To intervene if there is chaos or uncertainty on the court. You might give your setter her assignment, or tell the team what to do next.
4. To ice an opponent's server
5. To reiterate assignments that are not being carried out (regardless of the score)
6. A combination of 1-5

I would like to offer some suggestions for additional reasons for the use of time-outs.

7. What if we took time-outs to congratulate our team for things they're doing well? A quick time-out to remind them that what they're doing is working and why, can be very beneficial. Added benefit of such a time-out can be that it is sure to leave the other team confused as to who just took the time-out and why. Of course, when your team is 'hot' and has a ton of momentum, that's probably not a good time to take them out of their rhythm. But when the score is going back and forth, there is nothing wrong with re-emphasizing what's working.
8. Taking a time-out when your team just scored also has the benefit of preparing for the next play coming at you. You can adjust your

block and defense and talk about your opponent's most likely path of attack. If you're like me, you probably really enjoy this part of the game. We get to be fortune tellers, predicting who might get the ball and scheming how to defend it. Isn't it ironic that these moments usually come when we are serving, which probably means our opponent has taken the time out? If we take them ourselves, a time-out would probably fall earlier in a streak and could be the reason our streak gets going in the first place. After all, one point earned on our own serve (a mini-break) could be the only difference you need in a set if we side-out the rest of the way.

9. Or how about a time-out to re-center our own servers? You probably have them too; the servers that go on runs and serve with more and more risk every next serve? The odds of an ace increase, but so does the chance of an error. These servers often tend to terminate their own serving opportunities. Sometimes, a time-out after the third or fourth serve (that might have only barely made it over) can re-center them, while allowing you to set up your blocking scheme against the side-out.

2. Substitutions

Perhaps the most difficult decision that a coach has to make is when to replace a player with a teammate on the bench. It is also the most critical decision. If you wait too long, the set (or match) might be out of reach. If you do it too early, you might ruin the odds of your starter coming out of her funk and finding her stride. The college environment in the US is very concerned with the number of opportunities that exist for athletes. We are allowed 15 substitutions, for example, which caused our roster sizes to go up and has encouraged specialization in our sport beyond anything that's happening in the international arena. Don't get me wrong; I'm actually a huge fan of the 15 substitutions rule. If I were coaching the national team, I'd probably feel differently, but as a college coach, I enjoy the specialization and added opportunities to explore the use of defensive specialists and the various systems with 2 setters.

But with the added opportunities to make substitutions also comes the problem of interrupting the flow of the game.

While some players have no problems playing only three out of the six rotations, others struggle with their rhythm and it really affects their game. This is a problem that can partially be solved through savvy recruiting, but it should also factor into a coach's substitution habits.

When I started out coaching, I was much more concerned with keeping all of my players happy. This is of course the biggest pitfall of coaching: the very concept of everyone being happy is impossible to achieve.

I was bending over backwards to work people into the lineup by creating serving opportunities and DS roles. And I was very quick on the trigger by immediately replacing someone if they struggled at any point during a match. While I wasn't wrong by wanting to be fair to everyone, I've learned to be much more patient since then. I've realized that my first responsibility is to support the team that I put on the court and to give them the best chance to be successful. My way to provide them with that support is to give them the chance to fight off a sluggish start or to work though some trouble. As I said earlier in this chapter, as a coach the last thing I want is for my team to look at me after every mistake, afraid of making another one or of being taken out. And ironically, there might be benefits to our bench players as well. You may remember that vicarious experience (watching others perform successfully) has a positive correlation with confidence. If our bench watches the starters fight through a rough patch in a match and succeed, research suggests that actually may *increase* their own confidence.

I am now perhaps the opposite of how I coached in those early days. Perhaps I should make substitutions more quickly, especially if I have capable players on the bench. But I feel that the sign of trust I'm sending my team is worth taking the chance that I'm too late. My way to provide playing time and fairness to everyone on the roster these days looks a lot like the rotation philosophy many of the top European soccer clubs have adopted. As long as your roster is balanced, it makes sense to rotate players into the lineup and perhaps even have a set rotation. For example, Suzy plays the first match and Kelly the second and whoever performs best gets the third match.

I've started experimenting with this and I've found that it helps with competitiveness. But perhaps even more importantly, it also helps spread the physical burden that the Division III volleyball schedule places on our athletes. It is absolutely crazy and irresponsible how jam-packed our schedules are compared to every other level of volleyball. Our athletes are asked to play up to four complete best-of-five matches in an 18-hour time span on the weekends, sometimes back to back. Wouldn't it be nice if we could alleviate the physical demands on our players a little, while also sending our team the message of trust we want them to feel?

3. Line-up Adjustment

One of the most frustrating things but also fun things for a coach can be the adjustment of lineups from set to set. There are many different reasons to start a set a certain way. Most coaches have a favorite rotation they use to determine how to start and a team might get used to that. For us, it's rotation 3, when our setter is middle front. This rotation puts our L1 in left front, where she can take the first swing *and* it also puts our strongest server at the service line incase we start the match serving (which we always try to do). But there might be pressing reasons to change it up from time to time.

- It might be smart to match a certain blocker up with an attacker you're trying to slow down. If this is the case, you'll want to start in a rotation where your blocker starts out in the same zone as the opponent's attacker.
- Another possibility is that you might want to avoid your own blocker versus a certain attacker. That's the case with many coaches who have shorter setters in right front. The question then becomes which of the opponent's outside hitters you want to give the smaller block.

- A third scenario occurs in the fifth set. It is an unwritten rule that in those sets to 15, you start your hottest attacker in zone 4 (left front). It has been shown that this player will spend an average of 5-6 rotations in the front row, while someone who starts in right back, for example, can only count on an average of 3-4 rotations in the front row.

It is up to each coach to figure out which scenario is most important or which choices you'd like to make. Personally, I feel strongly about putting my best server on the service line. That's usually my first priority. But sometimes slowing down an opponent becomes more important and I might change it up, which is referred to as "spinning the dial". This is of course the most hilarious component of the game, because the other coach knows what I know and might spin the dial first, causing me to end up with the same matchup I was trying to avoid. It's the game of "I know that she knows that I know that she knows". The whole thing turns into a big game of chicken.

When I was in graduate school and coaching club volleyball on the side, I was known for my obsession with the details. Remembering that luck favors the prepared, I'd be out there during national qualifiers with a video camera, asking parents to videotape all of our possible opponents for the next day, hoping I'd get a glimpse of their starting lineups so I could adjust ours. I look back on my neurotic days with great fondness, but I've found a more stable outlook on the game. I've realized that most of the time, it's better to just focus on your own side of the net and not worry too much about what a coach on the other side might do. Don't get me wrong; I've spun the dial before just because I anticipated that the other coach would do it as well. But I've also learned to avoid paralysis by analysis.

On a related note, this is also why we have very limited use for video scouting in my program. In fact, our league has tried to institute video exchange for years, and I have not at all minded that it hasn't been done yet. Coaches like to watch video and can do it for hours, breaking down every little detail about an opponent. I once spent three days teaching my team that a particular outside hitter we'd see that weekend was mostly going to hit cross-court to the seam between zones 4/5. We practiced against it, we learned her name and her number, what perfume she liked to wear and what she liked to eat for breakfast. And when we played on Saturday, she absolutely killed us down the line. Tendencies are sometimes incredibly helpful and sometimes completely dependent on the opponent you're playing. If a block only gives you line, the video is going to show you hitting a lot of line. I like watching our opponents and watching for tendencies, but I try to stick to the big picture. Where are the holes in their defense, where are they vulnerable passing and what's their serving strategy? I've asked a few collegiate players who ended up playing for the national team what they remembered from their two-hour video sessions at practice, and to my surprise, the answer was usually "*very little*". Sometimes the game is the game and it just needs to be played. In the heat of the moment, you can remember the big things and everything else just needs to be duked out on the floor. I know that this sounds awfully black and white and that there is a level where video scouting is very helpful. But I'm convinced that most of us coaches have gone overboard in preparing our teams for specific opponents. I would much rather spend my energy on our own side of the net – there is more there that I hope I can control.

4. Post-match Feedback

I think one of the most overlooked priorities in volleyball is to have a clear goal going into every match. Especially at the Division III level, where we play three or four matches per weekend, in rapid succession, it can be hard to define a clear goal for every match. But it has to be done. How else can we sit down after a match and review with our teams?

We have all seen the huddles in the corner of the gym where coaches and teams are talking about the last match. How often are these meetings short and to the point? It seems to me that the longer the meeting, the more likely the team lost the match. I find it ironic that in moments of weakness and pain (over the loss), we spend more time reliving the cause of that feeling than we do in moments of jubilation and joy (over a win). Maybe it should be the other way around? When we win, it stands to reason we should explore why we were able to win and relish it. Whereas when we lose, well, sometimes less is more. I've discovered that I like to give my teams a quick synopsis of why I believe we won or lost and congratulate them on things that went well in the match, regardless of the outcome. It might be that our hitting percentage was great, or that we eliminated a lot of errors.

Or it's possible that we played with a lot of energy. There are usually positives to find after every match. In the case of a loss, it can also help to address reasons for the loss that do not have a direct relationship to your team. Maybe your opponents just played better than they usually do, or perhaps their outside hitter had the best night of her life.

By externalizing causes for a defeat, players can be helped explaining a result, while maintaining a high level of confidence (the positive explanatory style mentioned in chapter one). Then, it's on to the next match. If there are lingering issues, those can be addressed the next day at practice. That way our focus remains on the task in front of us because the most important ball is always the next one.

Of course these are just a few of the tools that we as coaches have at our disposal as we are trying to influence the outcome of games. And surely, serving and out of system theory are not the only topics that are important as we are training our teams to be successful. But I believe in keeping things simple. As coaches, it is important to send a consistent message and maybe tinker around the edges.

My players know the two pillars of our success are our serving game and how well we put pressure on our opponent out of system. They know what they can expect from me while I'm coaching them during games, and I believe this builds confidence. For you the pillars might be different, but I encourage you to build consistency into the message you're sending to your teams. Stay flexible and innovative by tinkering around those edges, but stay the course in terms of the technical and tactical building blocks of your program. I hope that you'll keep asking "*why not*" when carving out your own volleyball goals.

6

Recruiting and Team Composition

I always smile when I walk into the gym and some of my engineers are standing around the poles, debating how to set up the net in a more efficient manner. And I love making fun of them for it. It's ok, because they like to make fun of me, too. Mostly when I engage in philosophical monologues about the game, often right before ending practice so that all they can think about is how to get me to shut up so they can leave. We have a great relationship that way – based on the mutual understanding of our quirkiness.

It's made me think a lot about the types of players that are best suited to be coached by me within our system. It's not for everyone. All coaches are different and so recruiting players has to be different for everyone. I have heard coaches talk about the different roles that players can have on a team. These roles can vary from stud to stabilizer and everything in between. The argument commonly goes that a team has to be the right mix of these roles. You can't have a team full of studs, or a team of stabilizers alone.

There is certainly a lot to be said for the argument that there is only room for one Tom Brady on a team, instead of 11 of them. And I can see how 11 Messi's on a soccer team would never pass the ball to anyone. But rather than giving my own version of the role argument on teams, I'd like to explore the personalities behind these players, regardless of the role they have on the team. I don't necessarily believe that a team could not exist of a collection of all "studs" or all "stabilizers", but I believe that for this to happen, they'd have to have different personalities. Let me explain...

Those with a chip on their shoulder

When I started my job at Clarkson, I decided to go check out the local volleyball scene. I had heard through the grapevine that there was a local talent who was head and shoulders above everyone else in New York's section X. Her name was Sara and it made sense I would go see her play. Word on the street was that she would be the first girl to go play Division I, and coaches I had called had raved about what the girl could do. I remember going to the local high school when Sara's team came to visit, and watching the teams warm up.

I introduced myself to Sara's coach who asked me to give her an honest evaluation of her player's potential so that she could advise the family better. *"In fact"*, she said, *"why don't you call her after the game and tell her what you think."* I had just rolled out of a job as a recruiting coordinator for a mid-major Division I program, so she felt like I was a great objective resource. It took me only 5 minutes to have my opinion ready for her after watching her pepper and hit. Sara was a 5'9 skinny girl with a fast arm, but she had grown up in an environment where she had to teach herself how to play volleyball.

I later learned that Sara's mom had put up a net in their back yard where Sara could practice hitting jump serves. The yard had a significant slope to it, so she had to be careful to only serve up hill, so that she wouldn't spend the majority of her practice time chasing the ball. But she didn't have a choice; it was the only place where she was allowed to practice her jump serves. If she did it at practice, her teammates weren't able to return anything. So her coach forbade her to even try it. Under hand only for everyone! Sara was obviously talented, and racked up kill after kill in the match that I watched. But the level of volleyball was so low and the experience factor so against her, that I could not see her achieving her Division I goal. Now came the fun part: My promise to her coach that I would share my evaluation with Sara. I called her the next day. This is roughly how the conversation went…

Johan: "Sara, I have heard you want to play Division I volleyball. I coached at that level for quite a few years. Would you like my opinion?"

Sara: "absolutely – what do you think?"

Johan: "well, you are obviously talented – you have above average arm speed and jump fairly well, but at this point I think you have to be realistic and look at other options as well."

Sara: "you don't think I can do it?"

Johan: "well, I'm going to be objective – I'm not even sure you would play here at Clarkson. If you applied here, I think you'd make the team, although I'm not 100% sure. But I'm sure I've pissed you off enough to where you won't consider Clarkson anymore. That's ok – I just want you to start looking at some Division III schools so you don't end up missing out."

Sara: "Thanks for your time, Coach. I disagree with you, but I appreciate your time and honesty. Good luck to you."

I liked her immediately. What 16 or 17 year old has the wind taken out of her sails like that and stays completely courteous? I'm sure I wasn't her favorite person in the world by a long shot, but I was not trying to be liked and in the process probably gave Sara the first honest objective evaluation of her volleyball career.

Ironically, a little over a year later, Sara enrolled at Clarkson and became a member of my team. The year between our first meeting and her initial enrollment, she had come to our summer camps, attended clinics we ran at local high schools, and took every opportunity available to her to learn more about the game. For Sara, it wasn't personal – she just wanted to get better and had decided if she could use me for that purpose, she would - even if she didn't like me very much initially. I didn't blame her -you could say that I had in essence done everything I could to turn her against me. Ironically, that only made her more intent on proving me wrong. Four years later, Sara left Clarkson as the most decorated player to have ever attended the school – a 3-time AVCA All-American and conference Player of the Year in her senior year. She may not have been able to do that in Division I, but she was determined to make me eat my words about her not even making my own team. To me she will always be that player with a chip on her shoulder, determined to prove the world that a skinny 5'9 outside hitter from St. Regis Falls, NY can –as the Dutch saying goes- hit to make more than just a dent in a stick of butter.

My first recruiting rule is that I want as many of these players as I can get. There is no limit on them. I want those determined girls who are out to prove the world – and sometimes *me* – wrong. There have been many. We made Rachel come back on an unofficial visit after scolding her about her inappropriate cell phone use on her official visit and telling her we weren't sure she'd fit in very well. She ended up as one of the best team captains I've ever had the pleasure of coaching. There was Alison, the libero who barely got a sniff of the court as a DS for her club and broke every defensive record as a libero for our first NCAA tournament team. There was Victoria, who was told by her club coach that she wouldn't be of much value as an attacker no matter where she went. She might have even started believing it, until she was voted Conference Rookie of the Year while taking her Clarkson team to the Elite Eight as a starting outside hitter. There was Lani, who was told by the #2 Division II team in the country at the time that she was too short to play front row as a setter. It's true, Lani's block is not the most fear-inspiring you've ever seen, but her grit and determination ended up making Lani an All-American as a sophomore. She's been to three NCAA tournaments as a starting setter running a 5-1 offense. And I'll never forget Erika, who lost the battle for the starting setter position in her freshman year to Lani and asked if she could then perhaps be our libero. We had major doubts and told her the odds were very slim that was going to work out. Then our starting libero transferred and two years later Erika is perhaps the best libero to have ever played at Clarkson. The list goes on and on. It's not always about talent alone – I'm convinced it's just as much about the mindset behind it.

Leaders and Followers

Any team needs both leaders and followers. Too many captains on a ship and a power struggle is bound to break out, just as too many worker bees without a queen tend to buzz around aimlessly before perishing as a group. The thing about leaders that provides a challenge in the recruiting process is that sometimes leaders have to be developed over time. In your recruiting cycle, it's then important to consider whether you need someone to instantly take charge or whether you already have a leader whom they could be mentored by for a season or two.

I'm not sure where I stand in the nature/nurture debate on leaders. Are they born or taught to be leaders? I think there are great arguments to support both and the truth might be somewhere in the middle. What I am certain about is that for those who possess the potential to lead, that ability needs to be harnessed and developed much like athletic potential. Our setter for our first NCAA-bound team always considered herself a leader and she definitely possessed some of the character traits that you would normally attribute to good leaders. But it wasn't until the 2009 season that she was able to get her team to follow her. It was a combination of commanding respect based on behavior as well as articulating the goals for the program. She was good in both categories, but especially outstanding in the latter. Our goals to win a championship and reach the NCAA tournament were such a burning desire for Jenna, that it was hard not to get excited about following her. She went from a girl taking a walk to a great leader. It just took some time.

Introverts and Extraverts

There are many coaches out there who will tell you that certain positions require certain personalities. More often than not, this is based on personal preferences. Should your libero be loud and talkative on the court? Should your setter? Instinctually, I would have always answered both with a resounding "yes", but lately I've come to nuance that opinion. I've coached outstanding liberos who were more reserved and introverted, while I've seen outstanding setters in that category as well. I think the true difficulty lies in selecting a careful balance of introverts and extraverts and not so much in assigning specific positions to those personalities. I believe every team needs the rah-rah cheerleader but I've learned that this player doesn't necessarily have to be on the court very much.

Perhaps it's better to categorize your team along the "energy giver spectrum". I like to look at my players as "givers", "takers" or "neutrals". If you have an energy taker on your team, you're in trouble. Those are typically the players who are not well respected, and whose mere presence on the court causes everyone else to perform worse. They're the drama queens of the team or the rule breakers that no one respects. Sometimes a coach doesn't know right away why, but gradually hopefully we come to see that we have them; the energy hogs. Priority number one is to get them off the court. Priority two might be to get them off the roster.

The neutrals are more interesting. Most teams have a bunch of them. They are the players who don't show emotion very easily and probably don't really communicate. Keep in mind, though, that communicating can happen in a lot of ways. I have players who communicate confidence by just doing their jobs and their teammates feel their presence rather than hear them. They are still giving energy. Energy neutral players are those players who simply "exist" on the court. The way I know if someone is a "neutral" is by asking myself the following question: If we win, would I be able to tell how much the player contributed to the win. And if we lose, how likely would it be that I would attribute some of the blame to this player's behavior. If it's more likely I would attribute blame, then she's probably energy neutral.

It's not a bad thing to be energy neutral. Every team needs to have a stabilizing personality, who's more even-keeled and introverted and could perhaps be an energy neutral player. At a school with a very science-oriented curriculum, it is sometimes easier to find the more introverted players, so during my recruiting I have to be very conscious to look for the right amount of outgoing personalities. I've learned to stop worrying about what position they play.

It's important to have the right balance of athletes on the court. Too many neutrals and you could be in danger of lack of communication, or lack of passion – both recipes for losing. Generally, the more givers, the more you're going to like your win/loss record.

Clowns and Frowns

The argument that balance of personalities is more important positional characteristics holds true for another crucial trait as well. I believe successful teams have the ability to fend off stress and difficult situations with a team sense of humor. These teams rely on the team "clowns", the players who provide the sarcasm and the comedic outlet. It's often these players that have a very good sense of what individual team members appreciate and what they need. They don't allow sarcasm to get out of hand, or humor to become disrespectful, but rather keep a great balance between fun and carefree on one hand and focused on the other. It's especially unique and helpful if the team clowns are on the same wavelength as their coach, thereby connecting the coaching staff with the team. At Clarkson, it has become a team tradition to put the coaching staff on the spot at team dinners on long road trips. I'm certain tons of coaches around the country can relate to having to endure this: Each year that we've taken a long trip (where we fly to our destination), my players have told wait staff at our restaurants that it's my birthday, soliciting the traditional ice cream or cake with candles along with singing waitresses.

Of course my actual birthday isn't anytime close to our playing season, but my team has decided that they find this hilarious, and I've become very fond of it as well. It's a tradition that's been past on from team to team. Apparently there is a something about seeing your coach dance the funky chicken to a birthday song while wearing a gigantic blue sombrero. I stopped asking questions a long time ago – humor is a powerful facilitator of team unity.

Winners and Beginners

Regardless of what level your recruits have played at, some of them have learned what it takes to win and some have never had the lucky circumstance of tasting success. Now, the best players sometimes play on not-so-talented teams and do just fine. But I'm convinced that if your team is going to perform well under pressure, at the very least it helps to have a majority of players on your roster who have been in stressful situations before and prevailed. This experience can mean the difference between faltering in the conference championship match and pulling out an upset victory.

The PhD Factor

To be sure, your players' experiences with being successful under pressure do not need to have taken place in the athletic arena.

When I'm recruiting, I am fond of asking the question *"what was the hardest thing you've ever had to do?"* I've had a variety of very good answers to the question. It doesn't always tell me what I want to know. But every once in a while when the answer involves something about who to choose for a prom date, or having had to sit on the bench for a game or two, I might be tempted to be careful before I would put someone like that at the service line at match point in a regional championship match. A very respected collegiate soccer coach once referred to it to me as the "PhD Factor". PhD stands for "poor, hungry and driven." This of course refers to those who have had to work hard and fight for their success and are motivated to remain or become successful. It's no coincidence that my favorite recruits and some of my best players had their "doctorate".

No Substitute for Sincerity

Our search for players is never-ending. Each year we try to find the best possible fit for our team and the best complement for our current group of personalities. We are always on the look-out for the players with the chip on their shoulder. I've found that in this process, brutal honesty and sincerity are my biggest allies. Some recruiters live by the principle that we recruit in poetry but coach in prose. I'm not sure I buy into that. By giving prospects a brutal analysis of their game and potential fit for our program I open myself up to potentially being wrong. But I've learned that if I am wrong, sometimes that's the best thing that could've happened. Just thinking back to Sara's development into an All-American makes me realize that the benefits to challenging young athletes far outweigh the drawbacks. You end up with the players that don't back down. Not only that; with a little luck, you start off the player-coach relationship with the understanding that the brutal truth is the standard between you. In my mind, that's a very healthy situation.

The example that comes to mind is a girl named Amanda. Amanda would cringe if she knew I just called her by her first name because she was "Rank" to everyone, including the coaches. Rank stands out as the most challenging athlete I've ever coached. Not because she was so unpleasant, but rather because she was so brutally honest. Rank was one of the freshmen who wanted to speed up our .500 goal and that was no surprise to me. I recruited her because, even though she wasn't the typical setter/libero as far as her personality, she knew exactly what she wanted and would tell you, too. And it's hard to find that trait in anyone.

Rank and I communicated on an almost daily basis through e-mail while she was a senior in High School. She had a rough year, worrying about her brother's deployment in Iraq, and was looking for a good home where she could feel like she was part of a family. But she was also a winner: Wherever she ended up, the standards had to be high. And she wasn't afraid to speak up about what she was looking for. Rank let me know, for example, that she wanted a coach who would take cell phones away on the road and that she had no patience for excuses of any kind. I could only assume she probably was this honest with other coaches who were recruiting her as well. My hunch was confirmed when Rank forwarded me a copy of an e-mail she had just sent to a rivaling school that had been hot on her trail. It told that particular coach straight up that she hated his coaching style and would never play for him. Just like that, with absolutely no beating around the bush, this 17-year old girl told a very seasoned coach that she wasn't impressed and had other plans for herself. Ultimately, my decision that she was the one I wanted for my team had as least as much to do with the e-mail she sent to the other coach as with her setting and defensive skills. I figured I would never have to worry about Amanda not telling me the truth. And Lord knows, I certainly never had to. In retrospect coaching Amanda was one of the most rewarding coach/player experiences I've had in my career thus far.

Of course, there is another huge advantage of being completely upfront when it comes to communicating about a recruit's role that we foresee her having. It allows our recruits to get a good idea of how they would fit in.

We make sure we tell them at all times where they stand and how many other girls we are looking at. One of the drawbacks to recruiting in Division III is that we don't have a "signing date" where our incoming players commit to us and we to them. Instead, more often than not, we have to wait for financial aid packages to come out, at which point families make their decisions. This creates a first come, first served scenario of who commits first.

Some coaches I know will allow as many players as possible to commit, and will hold tryouts in the fall. This would allow for the possibility where you choose your school hoping to play volleyball, and then get cut from the team on the first day of preseason. In my opinion, this does more harm than good. If a relationship is to start out on the right foot, then it's our job as coaches to be a little bit more prudent with how we add players to our teams. In my case, I only have a limited number of players apply. They are those who have visited and who liked us as much as we liked them. They might still have other schools they're looking at, but we are in their top two or three. And I might have two or three of them on my list. Once financial aid comes out, these players are told exactly how many players we will take and who is number 1, 2 or 3 on our list. That way, they have all the information they need to make a solid decision. And being told you're number 3 on the list isn't necessarily as bad as it sounds, because each of these recruits has received an evaluation of what we believe they can do when they're here and we believe all of them can be successful or we wouldn't be recruiting them. I've also told recruits that they may have to be patient for a few years while they learn the ropes of the collegiate game before expecting playing time. And we've certainly told players that we saw their role initially as practice players. We have lost recruits because of our recruiting strategy, and I've gone into seasons with only two middles on the roster, or only one setter.

But ultimately I believe it's the only way to get the players that are truly committed to what you have to offer them. The ones who got not-so-good news might come and try to prove you wrong, while the top recruits know that they weren't part of a group of seven or eight "top recruits". Either way, you end up with recruits that are as committed to you as you are to them.

Building Relationships

With limited resources, I can't afford to scour the earth looking for these players.

Instead, I rely heavily on coaches and recruiters that I know and who know me. Sincerity is the key here as well, because there has to be a level of trust there before you can rely on others for the future of your program. One of my early-career mentors was fond of saying, "*trust comes on foot but leaves on horseback.*" His warning will remain with me forever. The application to my job is that it's important to be truthful, rather than promise athletes things you can't deliver, thereby deceiving them. And the people who will refer players to my program hopefully know that Clarkson does things the right way. Going to recruiting tournaments for me, then, is sometimes less about finding players than it is about rekindling my relationships with my eyes and ears in the volleyball world: my contacts. It might sound strange, but it's been a very effective way of recruiting. I enjoy discussing the game with my high school and club colleagues as much as I do finding a great player for my program and as it turns out, the two go hand in hand.

Addition by Subtraction

Team composition is about the delicate balance of mixing the right personalities. In that process, it's crucially important to not just have eye for which personalities you'd like to *add* to the group, but also which need to be *removed* from it. Looking back on the many teams I have coached at several levels of competition, I feel comfortable saying that I've never seen a team succeed in achieving its goals if individuals' personalities got in the way. I'm thinking of the players who consider their own ego's more important than team success, or those who like to complain and gossip as well as players who are quick to make excuses and are often dishonest in doing so.

Each team usually has someone who shows some of these characteristics, and sometimes a team can contain it. But I'm convinced that there certainly can never be more than one. Interestingly enough, my most successful teams have been the ones where the troublemakers had been cut or chose to leave. You see, a team can be successful despite lack of talent, but it can never be successful with a lack of character. It's not always about cutting the least talented players from a team. Sometimes it's about cutting a certain personality from the team so that you end up with the right mix. When I was starting out as a coach, I was sometimes blinded by the talent factor, thinking I could help someone see the light on things like work ethic, honesty and her ability to be a good teammate. After 13 years of coaching, I have to say that has completely changed. If someone doesn't pull her weight off the court and consistently creates issues, the decision to cut that player is a necessary one. After all, the purpose of the program is bigger than any one individual athlete (or coach).

7

The Purpose of a Program with Purpose

The rise of the Clarkson volleyball program is the most extraordinary thing I have ever been a part of. Because deep down I am deathly afraid of being ordinary, it was my intent to write down my experiences to remember them forever. I am hoping it'll serve as a reminder of how far we've come and how hard we have to work to protect and expand upon our success. I want to guard against complacency at all times. I also wanted to make sure future and former players would have the chance to read about how our project came to be and how our decisions and beliefs have enabled it to be successful. I hope that the result of this effort can perhaps aid you in thinking about how to build your program or team. This is not a book with mostly drills and technical advice but rather a description of those elements of our program that I believe paved the way for us to have the success that we did. It is quite possible that perhaps they make us a little different than some of the other programs out there.

We are probably different in a lot of ways, and I am often reminded of this when, in the middle of a heated time-out, my players look at me and say, "*Coach, you made that word up*". But it's not just my inability to hide my accent in times of stress that makes us different. Nor is it the bizarre pregame speeches and motivational quotes that teams with Dutch coaches sometimes get to endure. Among them there have been opened cans of whoopass, ninja sharks named Bruce, flashlights in the dark, countless bears with fleas, and trampled elephants. Most of all, I believe we are different because of how we go about chasing our common goals. I take great pride in the bond that exists between all of us who chose the unique combination of standards and priorities described in this book and by doing so became part of the Clarkson volleyball family.

It is reassuring to me that after all is said and done, there is no one single truth in volleyball. There are many ways to pass a volleyball, and as many variations to hitting technique and teaching blocking. Many ways lead to Rome and ultimately whether you are successful or not depends at least as much on decisions that have absolutely nothing to do with hand positioning and jumping ability. It was my intention to offer some suggestions of things to ponder in terms of structuring your own program when it comes to priorities on and off the court. It was my goal to perhaps help you think of some ways to achieve those goals that deal with communication, goal setting, support building, and recruiting. The single most important element in all of this remains *purpose*; knowing why you make the decisions you make and standing by them. The Dutch don't believe in wishing anyone "good luck". After all, luck should have nothing to do with the outcome. Instead they wish you *"much success"*. So I'm wishing you *"much success"* as you strive for your next championship. Coaching is such a great profession. We get to truly create our own universe and the result can be an incredibly rewarding experience. Just as long as they don't replace the championship trophy with a box of crayons...

About the Author

In his first seven years at Clarkson, Johan Dulfer has transformed the Golden Knights volleyball program into a regional power-house and launched it onto the National Scene. Inheriting a program that won just 7 matches in 2006, Dulfer turned the program's fortunes around in just one season, by going 23-17 the next year. The definitive regional breakthrough came in 2009, when Clarkson won its first-ever conference title and advanced to the NCAA tournament for the first time in school history. Since 2009, Clarkson has racked up a .779 win percentage, boasting four consecutive NCAA appearances, 2 conference tournament titles and 2 regular season championships. In 2012, Clarkson played its way to a program best 31 wins en route to the National Quarterfinals. The Golden Knights also gained their first-ever national ranking at the end of that season.

Dulfer, a two-time Liberty League coach of the year, came to Clarkson from James Madison University where he spent three years as the first assistant and recruiting coordinator. During his time in Harrisonburg, the Dukes were 45-36 and made two CAA tournament appearances. Prior to his stint in Harrisonburg, Dulfer was the student assistant at the University of Minnesota, helping the Golden Gophers to the Big Ten Championship in 2002 under the tutelage of dr. Mike Hebert.

A native of the Netherlands, Dulfer has served as one of the assistant coaches and program director of the Iroquois-Empire High Performance Program in New York, and has also coached several touring international club teams. Dulfer received a master's degree in both Kinesiology, with an emphasis in Sport Psychology, from the University of Minnesota in 2003, and a master's degree in International Relations & Propaedeuse in Dutch Law from the University of Groningen (the Netherlands) in 1999.

Made in the USA
Lexington, KY
24 October 2013

26992461R00080